Also
A
Poet

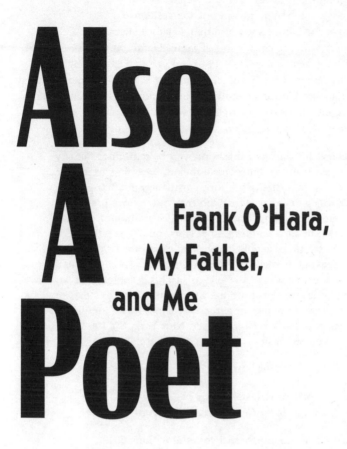

Also A Poet

Frank O'Hara, My Father, and Me

ADA CALHOUN

Grove Press
New York

Also
A
Poet

Chapter 1

My childhood home was a top-floor walk-up apartment in Lower Manhattan. By the time I was born, most of the bohemians belonging to my parents' downtown scene had decamped to suburbs or college towns—or at least to elevator buildings on the Upper West Side. Even I left New York for a few years. But my parents remained in their East Village apartment, decade after decade.

In the fall of 2018, I popped by to look for a toy to give my baby goddaughter. In the warren of their building's basement, my parents stored papers, books, and bubble-wrapped appliances—not antique so much as just old and unused. That afternoon, I went through the small, tiled lobby, past a padlocked door, and down narrow metal stairs into the dank space, ten degrees cooler than the hall. I hit my head and cursed myself for doing it. On the rare occasions I've gone into the basement since I reached five foot nine in high school, I've reminded myself not to stand up straight, and every single time I've forgotten and smacked my head on a ceiling pipe.

In a heavy filing cabinet almost as tall as I am, I found what I'd come for—my old miniature plastic foods for playing kitchen, in storage since I'd graduated to a Spirograph and Sit 'n Spin thirty-five years earlier.

Then I noticed something in another of the heavy drawers that, in my haste to spend no more time in the basement than necessary, I hadn't seen before: dozens of loose, dust-covered cassette tapes labeled with the dates 1977 or 1976, the year I was born, along with names like Willem de Kooning and Edward Gorey. I'd never met any of these people, but I knew their names. They were painters and poets—people it would make sense for my father—Peter Schjeldahl, an art critic—to have known.

Before I was born, he'd been a hotshot poet, giving readings at crowded galleries, lofts, and churches in Manhattan. His inspiration both for writing and for moving to New York City was his idol: the poet Frank O'Hara.

O'Hara wasn't as famous a cultural figure of the midcentury as the Beatles or Andy Warhol, but to people who cared about art and literature he and his cohort of cosmopolitan New York City poets and painters were the ones you would push past more famous people to get to. They ushered in a lusty new gay sensibility—urbane, witty, obsessed with all forms of culture from Russian ballet to the trashiest Hollywood movies. O'Hara was the group's beating heart.

In his early twenties, my father met O'Hara, sixteen years his senior, a few times at parties. With his crooked nose and wide smile, high forehead and light blue eyes, O'Hara looked soft and hard at the same time: part boxer, part librarian. He was short, but thanks to his perfect posture and a tendency to walk on the balls of his feet, he seemed taller. The last time my father saw him, O'Hara inscribed a catalog to him at a Museum of Modern Art opening: "for Peter with palship from Frank."

A month later, on July 25, 1966, O'Hara died at the age of forty in a freak vehicular accident on Fire Island, a gay-friendly vacation town off the South Shore of Long Island known for being car-free. A beach taxi he and his friends were taking from a dance bar to the house they were staying in broke down. While they were waiting for another taxi in the darkness, O'Hara was hit by a dune buggy driven by a young man on a date. In my father's obituary for the *Village Voice*, he wrote: "Everything about O'Hara is easy to demonstrate and exceedingly difficult to 'understand.' And the aura of the legendary, never far from him while he lived, now seems about to engulf the memory of all he was and did."

The less affectionate *New York Times* obituary, which appeared with no byline, is riddled with an impressive number of errors, given its brevity. Among other things, it said O'Hara was hit by a taxi, not a dune buggy, and it gave his address as that of Grace Church's churchyard—not a likely residence for a lapsed Catholic. Worse, it minimized O'Hara's literary importance, suggesting he was little more than a museum functionary and a muse who posed for a scandalous painting by the abstract expressionist painter and troublemaker Larry Rivers. The headline identified him as a museum curator; the subheadline: "EXHIBITIONS AIDE AT MODERN ART DIES—ALSO A POET."

My father, long-haired and glassy-eyed, wearing spats and a dandyish vest with pockets for his pocket watch and pillbox of amphetamines, spent the rest of the sixties and early seventies staying out late, he said, so he had time to make the maximum number of mistakes.

At an art opening at the Whitney Museum in 1973, he met my mother, Donnie Brooke Alderson. She'd recently retired from musical touring shows like *You're a Good Man, Charlie Brown*. (No one who knew her would be surprised to hear she'd played Lucy.) She'd spent a good part of the sixties working as a hostess on a cruise ship. On one voyage, she had a mystical experience while staring out at the ocean, a cigarette in one hand and a beer in the other.

Now in New York, working with her accompanist, Gary Simmons, she'd begun doing stand-up comedy in lesbian bars. A Texas girl, she never went to a party without full makeup and high heels, and she still carried herself like the ballet dancer she once was. As a child, she'd appeared as Clara in *The Nutcracker* alongside America's first major prima ballerina, Maria Tallchief.

My father didn't know much about dance, but he would have known that name. In a marriage poem for his friends Jane Freilicher and Joe Hazan, "Poem Read at Joan Mitchell's," Frank O'Hara wrote that Maria Tallchief's rhinestones heralded spring.

When I was born, my father gave up sleeping until noon but otherwise carried on as before, writing all day and drinking all evening. He didn't write poetry anymore, but he did poetically write art criticism for the *New York Times*, *Art in America*, and the *Village Voice*.

Over time, even though he was a college dropout and in many respects sort of a mess, he became one of the most respected art critics in the country. His meticulously crafted sentences require many of his fans to keep a dictionary by their side when they read him. And yet, he wasn't pedantic or academic. He wrote as a fan, full of love of and enthusiasm for beauty. His reviews were so persuasive they could make readers see even Picasso and Rembrandt in a new way.

After climbing the four flights to my parents' apartment, I asked my father about the tapes I'd found in the basement.

"They're interviews I did in the seventies," he said, and grimaced. "I was going to write a biography of Frank O'Hara."

I'd always loved Frank O'Hara's poetry. I copied his style when I wrote poetry myself as a bookish little girl, and I've given many friends copies of his book *Lunch Poems* over the years. There was something about his poems that made me feel like I was sharing a wonderful secret. A verse about how a drink tasted or a city block looked felt like an invitation to another world. An O'Hara poem could make even public-school hallways shimmer with possibility.

My father said that looking at those tapes made him depressed. By not finishing the biography, my father felt he'd let down his hero. He wrote of O'Hara in the *New York Times* in 1974: "He seems to have had that most dubious and enchanting of gifts, the ability to romanticize reality, for oneself and others, as it is happening. His legend, an inextricable tangle of fact and inflated memory, is going to be with us for a long time."

O'Hara's legacy haunted my father and inflected his sentences. People noticed. In the *New Criterion*, art critic Roger Kimball wrote: "In many respects, Mr. Schjeldahl's style is a demotic and more dour version of Frank O'Hara's, the poet-critic upon whom he has most conspicuously modeled himself."

I took the tapes home and put one into my cassette player. Suddenly I was standing in a Soho loft, drink in hand, watching my handsome, strung-out young father up at the front of the room.

Peter Schjeldahl Reading—SoHo, New York City
(98 Greene Street)—3/1/71
Unknown voice: A poetry recital at the 98 Greene Street loft held on
    March 1, 1971. The poet is Peter Schendell [*sic*].
Peter Schjeldahl: *"La Vie en Rose."* For Larry Fagin.
To deal with death, ignore it.
Then when it shows up, feign madness.
Make faces.
It will be frightened and disappear.
[Crowd laughs.]

In the past decade I've spent writing books—a few under my own name and many more as a ghostwriter—I've seen projects fall apart for all sorts of reasons. Still, I couldn't imagine how anyone, especially a great writer embedded in the scene, could do that many interviews and have nothing come of it.

In the days after I found the tapes, I ransacked libraries, bookstores, and the Internet for everything I could find about O'Hara. I discovered that there was a hole in the canon where my father's contribution would have been. One book from 1979 about O'Hara's work even referenced his biography as a work in progress.

I invited my father out for lunch at our favorite diner, Odessa, so I could ask him about his doomed biography. Odessa sat a block and a half from my parents' apartment, on Avenue A, which runs along the western side of Tompkins Square Park. I once took an extremely famous person there for lunch and, to my satisfaction, the Odessa waitress was as gruff with his pierogi order as she was with everyone else's. Over eggs, I turned on my tape recorder and asked my father for the story of the O'Hara book.

Looking disheveled in messy hair, crooked glasses, and an unbuttoned plaid shirt over a gray T-shirt, my father hunched a little, as if still at his desk. He said the problem was the relationship he had with the estate's executor, O'Hara's younger sister, Maureen O'Hara Granville-Smith. He said initially she was in favor of his project, but then she kept putting him off when it came to making O'Hara's letters available. She would say she was mailing him copies and they wouldn't show up. She would say "soon," and then soon and even much later than soon would arrive and still no letters.

This went on for months and then more than a year, until finally he began to suspect that the material would never come. His agent, Maxine Groffsky, and his publisher, Harper and Row, tried to help him negotiate with Maureen, to do anything to keep the project alive, but evidently there was nothing he could do to change her mind. He was out as authorized biographer. At a tense lunch with his editor about returning the advance, he said he'd been through hell and should be allowed to keep the money—which, by the way, he had already spent. In the end, he was allowed to keep the first $7,500 of his $15,000 advance. The rest of the contract was canceled. The tapes went into the basement, and my father tried not to think about them again.

Sixteen years passed before the publication of the only significant O'Hara biography, *City Poet: The Life and Times of Frank O'Hara* by Brad Gooch, which came out in 1993. My father had theories about why Maureen decided he was wrong for the project and that, two decades later, Gooch was right. He came to believe that she was opposed to anything that might reflect poorly on the O'Haras. She seemed to fear, too, that O'Hara's homosexuality would be all anyone remembered of his story—and perhaps she had more cause to worry about that in the 1970s than in the 1990s.

The well-off O'Haras, who were what used to be called lace-curtain Irish, cared about appearances. Frank gave them trouble even before he was born by being conceived out of wedlock. O'Hara's parents moved to Baltimore soon after marrying. When they returned, they told everyone that their son had been born on June 27, 1926—three months later than his true birthday.

I'm not a believer in horoscopes, but there's still something unsettling about Frank O'Hara living his whole life believing he was a Cancer when really he was an Aries. My father thinks that when he started to ask questions about the birthday discrepancy was when Maureen began to freeze him out.

Peter Schjeldahl—Odessa Diner, East Village, New York City
(119 Avenue A)—11/9/18

Peter Schjeldahl: She started out super friendly, super cooperative, and then it got weird.

Ada Calhoun: And when did it get weird?

PS: Pretty soon. I mean, well, no, it's like— It was weird for a long time before I realized it was weird, you know? It was like nothing was happening and then there's this note of hostility. And then when I talked to the brother in Chicago and raised the question about the birth date, it became militant.

Sitting across from my father at Odessa, I listened with compassion. Still, I was pretty sure that whatever had happened, he must have been partly to blame. He'd always had a gift for accidentally saying terrible things. My mother said he should give out business cards that read: PETER SCHJELDAHL—BRIDGE BURNER. I imagined him throwing a handful of them into the air as he fled from a cocktail party where he'd just offended the host.

From a very young age, I knew that my father wasn't like the fathers on TV shows or in movies. He wasn't a protector or an advice giver. He took pride in always choosing freedom over security. Studying Martin Luther King Jr. circa 1985 at PS 41, I asked my father if he'd attended the 1963 March on Washington. He told me that he was assigned by his New Jersey paper to cover it, but he overslept and missed his bus. Later that day, he walked into the newsroom and saw his colleagues huddled around a black-and-white TV, trying to spot him in the crowd.

My takeaway from this story—and from most of the stories he told—was that I shouldn't count on him.

In rebellion against his flakiness, I became compulsively reliable. I don't think the Girl Scouts bivouacked in the 1980s East Village, but had they, I would have earned all the badges. Growing up, I was a hall monitor and teacher's pet. As an adult, I became friends' go-to executor on wills; godmother to children; reference writer for co-op board, adoption, and school applications. With my CPR/first aid/ AED certification current, I would give you directions, watch your bag while you made a call, and feed your cats while you were away. A *Village Voice* profile described me as "cheerful and mannerly." My credit score: 837. Excellent.

My father and I had just one thing in common: writing. I didn't particularly want to follow in his footsteps, but it felt fated. I learned to read early and went to the library every week for a new stack of books to haul up the stairs. In middle school, I memorized Shakespeare and Coleridge and edited the school paper. In my twenties, I became a newspaper reporter. In my thirties, I started writing books. At various points over the years, I tried to follow different paths—translator, photographer—but writing and editing seemed like what I was built for, like a greyhound is born to run.

Before I even started elementary school, I would wake up in the middle of the night with lines of poetry in my head. Preserved in a large manila envelope decorated with a penguin sticker, marker drawings of a tree, wreath, Santa, candy cane, and presents, plus a big "Do not open until Christmas," is a book of poetry by me called *City Poems*. Here's one:

A Summer Night in the City

Outside in the dark blue sky
Lights are glowing.
All of the lights are out
Except this very one
Where I am writing away at plans for a new day.
(Good night.)

I was six. At that age, I loved staying up late, looking out into the dark, seeing people go places. In the darkness, with no one watching me, I could be anything. And what I chose alone in my room, with all the choices in the world at my feet, was to imitate my father, who was imitating Frank O'Hara—all three of us writing poems about New York and nighttime and dreams. I mimicked my father's O'Hara reverence the way a boy learns how to shave from watching his father's face in the bathroom mirror.

And yet, my father has been considered the real writer, the tortured artist creating behind a locked door. I've been the hard worker, meeting deadlines over a laptop in coffee shops or on the couch with a child watching *Wonder Pets!* at my side. I've always been a mystery to my father and he to me. The main difference is that I've been fascinated by him, and he's often seemed to forget I was there.

This O'Hara book, though—this seemed like a time when he'd failed at something that I was pretty sure I could have nailed. Maybe my Frank O'Hara biography wouldn't have been as poetic or elegant as his Frank O'Hara biography, but by god it would have gotten done. In my twenty years as a journalist, I've successfully interviewed hundreds of people, including difficult celebrities in their four-star Los Angeles hotel suites, lawyers in sleepy Southern towns, and gang members at the sites of Brooklyn shootings.

I thought of how many books I'd conjured into being with less than a quarter of the material in that basement drawer. A few years ago, I got a call from my agent telling me that a celebrity needed someone to redo the twenty thousand words the first ghostwriter had done and then to finish the hundred-thousand-word manuscript in five weeks. I took the job. The book came out on time and hit the *New York Times* bestseller list.

A couple of years after that, I sensed that a memoir on which I was the ghost might be in jeopardy. The celebrity was making sounds about the pages not sounding quite right, a red flag. I asked for a sample of writing that worked. Then I spent hours mapping the grammar of that sample, line by line, onto each story I'd been told. That book came out on time, and it, too, hit the *New York Times* bestseller list.

Ghostwriting is a good name for this job. If you do it well, you remain invisible. You learn to think and write as the person you're helping, and to fall at least half in love with them. To be good at this work you must have boundless curiosity about the subject's internal world, the way you would if they were your crush.

I was certain that if I'd been named Frank O'Hara's authorized biographer, I never would have let the project fall apart. I also thought that the executor might have had understandable reasons for being cautious about careless people digging too deeply into her brother's childhood, which after all was her childhood, too. I wondered if my father even tried to find out why she was so protective.

"Did you ever ask to interview Maureen herself?" I asked.

"No," he said.

There's your first mistake, I thought.

By the time I found the O'Hara tapes forty years after they went into the basement, nearly every one of the people my father had interviewed was dead. But his shame endured: "I felt that the interviews were horrible, and I was horrible," he told me at Odessa. "They were a total failure."

I felt sorry for my shame-steeped father, but I also felt something like glee. I knew that there must be a way that I could resurrect this project. These dual impulses—to do something noble and to win—characterized my time a decade ago as a national news reporter. I'd be interviewing someone in Alabama or Idaho about a tragedy. Half of me would feel moved, would think, *Here, before me, is a fellow human being who is suffering.* The other part, the reporter, sensing that this scene would produce potent copy, would have just one word in her head: *Yessssss.*

I asked my father if it would be okay for me to take the tapes and try to finish his O'Hara book. I said that it would keep his research, vital to literary history, from rotting, unheard, in an East Village basement. And it would bring us together in a common purpose. The book would be good for him, good for me, and it would almost write itself.

He said I was welcome to try. He also said, "I didn't know you were a Frank O'Hara fan."

That stopped me dead in my tracks.

To me this seemed a little like not knowing your child was a vegan or a Theosophist or allergic to bees. Then again, for a few months in ninth grade I was a full-blown witch. Wearing thrift-store slips as dresses, my pentacle-clad friends and I dripped so much wax from our candles that we used it to build a scale model of the town of Twin Peaks. He never noticed that either.

As we finished our omelets, I showed him a book I'd found that collected stories about O'Hara told by his friends. My father opened it and read aloud from writer Patsy Southgate's account of the time she and O'Hara tried to sleep together.

"It occurred in August, a hot night in the early sixties," the story began. "In bed at night, one felt as if one were lying on a sale table in Klein's basement during a failure of air-conditioning." Southgate, who grew up in Washington, DC, a beautiful WASP, was surprised she had a night alone with O'Hara in the Hamptons, but "fate occasionally does throw one a fish."

They wound up driving drunk at dawn after a party to Larry Rivers's house, where they turned up Erik Satie as loud as they wanted (very loud). As they drank on the white sofa, they decided to go to bed together.

Southgate was "madly in love with him in a way, and afflicted with one of those simple cases of hot pants that love, in all its innocence and wisdom, brings on." They got naked under the covers and made out, admiring each other's bodies (his large penis seemed perfect, Southgate said, as it went "with his flamboyance"), until finally he told her that he couldn't go through with it because of her husband, the painter Mike Goldberg: "Mike's too good a friend of mine," he said. *Rats*, she thought, and yet she said lying there with him was "pure heaven." She'd never felt closer to anyone than she had to him that night.

My father concluded his dramatic reading. Then he did what he often did in those days—segued into talking about his friend Spencer.

Spencer is a young artist, poet, and critic in New York City. My father had spent a lot of time with him in the prior couple of years. I'd met him once or twice and found him to be engaging, handsome, and bright. And yet, my father's enthusiasm for the relationship at times struck me as over-the-top.

"Spencer is the best interviewer I've ever seen," my father said. "He's really terrific. It comes out of total research. I mean, he will have read every word you wrote before he talks to you. And you believe he really wants to know. He asked me: 'When did you start regarding language as material?'"

I said that sounded like a clever question, but I must not have been sufficiently effusive because then my father said, in what sounded like a reprimand: "Spencer thinks that in general you don't take to friends of mine."

I was quiet for a second, trying to remember if I'd ever been rude to Spencer.

"What did he base that on?" I asked. "One of your former best friends was the man of honor in my wedding." I mentally tallied a list of his closest friends over the years, many of whom I'd thought of as family. I realized that my father hadn't spoken to most of them in a long time.

"Who are your other good friends besides Spencer these days?" I said.

"That's all," he said. "I sit at my desk and smoke and play hearts online and when I've got a deadline I write. Otherwise, it's just my thoughts, which are self-consuming."

My father has always loved me. I know it for a fact. He's told me. He's told other people. But he's never seemed particularly *interested* in me. I've never commanded the attention and enthusiasm of a Spencer.

As a little girl, I had nightmares. Once, I woke up in the middle of the night and went into the living room to find my father there playing solitaire. I was sure he would be annoyed by the interruption and send me back to bed, but instead he invited me to play cards with him. We played by the light of a table lamp until I grew sleepy again. When I mentioned later how nice that had been, maybe the nicest memory I have of him from my childhood, he said he didn't remember it; he told me he might have been in a blackout.

More than once, he's said that before he got sober when I was sixteen, the worst hours of his day were between 3:00 p.m., when he stopped writing, and 5:00 p.m., when he let himself start drinking. For a dozen of those years, I arrived home from school around three. In those hours, I can't remember him once asking about my day, making me a snack, or helping me with my homework.

Most men of that generation didn't do such things, of course, whether they were in the East Village or the suburbs. And why would he? The world has rewarded his single-minded focus on work. When I say his name to people in the art world, their eyes grow soft with admiration.

"Oh, I *love* your father's writing," they say.

I say, "He will be happy to hear that. I'll tell him."

But if they keep talking about how great he is, I start to squirm.

★ ★ ★

"There's something to this Frank O'Hara book idea, right?" I asked my therapist when I saw her a few days after the Odessa lunch. She says things like "complexifying the narrative," and I love her very much.

"It *is* a good idea," she said cautiously. "Just make sure you get it in writing from your father that you can do this, or he might forget you're doing it and give the tapes to someone else. He might be giving them to you because he doesn't think they have any value."

"It's not like that," I said. "This is really good for both of us! It's not like he's going to give these tapes to Spencer or something. He wants *me* to have them."

Then, walking away from her office down Broadway, I had a visceral memory of being a kid and longing to know what it would be like to sit in the front seat of the car. I asked my parents for weeks if I could. Finally, one evening my mother was driving and my father said the passenger seat was mine. I was overjoyed. I bounded into the front and put on the seat belt, then looked out the coveted windshield—and was blasted in the face by the sun, which was setting right in my eyes. The whole ride I struggled to see out the window, but it was too bright. I realized then that my father had given me the seat because, for the moment, he didn't want to be in it.

In an episode of the TV show *Mad Men*, Don Draper recites O'Hara's poem "Mayakovsky." In the TV adaptation of Sally Rooney's *Normal People*, one character gives another an O'Hara collection. These are two of the poet's only appearances in the cultural mainstream of the past fifty years if you don't count a line of his that pops up now and then on Instagram:

Now I am quietly waiting for
the catastrophe of my personality
to seem beautiful again,
and interesting, and modern.

I think about that line so often. Maybe writing this book would make
my father's messiness, his catastrophic personality, seem beautiful to
me. And if I pulled it off, maybe for the first time in my life I would
seem interesting and modern to him.

Chapter 2

With the help of my husband, Neal, I digitized all the fragile cassettes so that even if the brittle tapes snapped at the end, the audio would be preserved for posterity. Then I began listening to one or two of the recordings per day.

Learning about Frank O'Hara made me feel giddy. Just as his poetry made me see the city's potential, so the stories about his life in New York made me see the streets through his eyes.

O'Hara was raised Catholic in the middle-class small town of Grafton, in central Massachusetts. He studied the piano and wanted to be a composer. In World War II, he enlisted in the navy and served as a sonar man on a destroyer, the USS *Nicholas*. On the G.I. Bill, he went to Harvard as a music major, but, while he was there, his interest shifted to poetry.

After graduating in 1950, he moved to New York City and started hanging out with abstract expressionist painters who were part of the circle known as the New York School. He fell in love with his new friends, and he fell in love with the city. As Mark Doty, O'Hara expert and poet, has said, if William Blake saw in every face he passed in London "marks of weakness, marks of woe," O'Hara saw possible dates.

O'Hara got a job at the front desk at the Museum of Modern Art in 1951. He told friends that he took the job so he could spend more time with the show that was up at the time—a Matisse retrospective. He eventually became an associate curator. As his abstract expressionist friends became more successful, he became a valuable emissary between them and the museum.

O'Hara banged out some of his best poems in fits of inspiration on his lunch hour using a demonstration Olivetti Lettera 22 typewriter perched on a stand out in front of a shop on Fifth Avenue near Rockefeller Center. He also wrote at his MoMA desk or on his Royal FP at home, sometimes while watching TV or talking on the phone. My favorite poem of his—my favorite poem ever—is 1957's "To the Harbormaster," in which the narrator's ship is headed into port but gets caught in—and what a great word—"moorings."

One of the earliest tapes, from the fall of 1976, was of an interview with Joe LeSueur. LeSueur, an editor and writer, lived with O'Hara as his roommate on and off for years. They weren't lovers for most of that time, but they hosted dinner parties together and people thought of them as a duo, even though they dated other people.

LeSueur was born in Mesa, Arizona, in 1924. When his father lost everything in the 1929 crash, the family moved out to California. His parents were strict Latter-day Saints, and claimed Brigham Young among their ancestors. One of his grandfathers was polygamous, with two wives and more than twenty children. "It's quite a nice background to get away from," he told my father. LeSueur seemed proud of having broken away from the church, the only one he knew in his family who had.

Joe LeSueur—New York City—11/22/76
Peter Schjeldahl: How did you happen to get out of it?

Joe LeSueur: By going queer. When I have any gay friends who grumble about how awful it is, I give them my "Be Glad You're Gay" speech, because it probably got you out of terrible middle-class things. It certainly did me. God knows I may have gone right along with it. Not that it's the worst life in the world, but it does shut you off from certain stimulating things in life that I wouldn't have wanted to miss.

He didn't believe in assimilation. He never liked the word "gay," preferring "cocksucker, queer, or pansy." LeSueur said O'Hara also felt it was important to affirm his homosexuality, to make sure no one tried to gloss over it. When straight people said, "I don't see difference," LeSueur would yell at them.

JL: Every so often, I would have to remind some of my straights that I'm queer and don't pull any shit on me and don't forget it. Like, Mike goes, "Oh, Joe, we don't mind!" I say, "What do you mean, you don't *mind*? I'm just going to *remind* you."

At a party, O'Hara and LeSueur took a sudden liking to each other and began making out. According to LeSueur, the artist Willem de Kooning looked into the room where LeSueur and O'Hara were fooling around and described the scene to other partygoers with a big smile on his face: "God damn it! I like that! Cocks in there, doing their thing!"

JL: I lived on Fiftieth Street. He lived on Forty-Ninth Street. So I started dropping by and seeing him. It wasn't an affair at all, you see.
PS: Well, was there any of that?
JL: Yes. But I wanted to make it clear that we weren't lovers, because if we'd been lovers, I'd have hoped he'd have written me some love poems! But he loved me, as I did him. And it's mysterious.

PS: It sounds like a good marriage. A good marriage isn't an affair either, as I've discovered.

JL: He made it clear that he was very attracted to me. He let me know he was. I didn't plan to move in with him. I came back from Tuxedo Park, where I'd gone to teach for two years. It was a fantastic experience. Fourth, fifth, and sixth graders. Fourth graders are the best, most interesting. Make sure Ada gets a good education in the early grades when they do phonetics. Your mind is trained then.

It's odd hearing my name on this tape. I was eight months old at the time. LeSueur segues from my phonics education to describing how in the summer of 1957 he and O'Hara did peyote out in Southampton with Larry Rivers. LeSueur had read Aldous Huxley's *Doors of Perception* and tried mescaline, but O'Hara had never done hallucinogens before. While tripping, they went and saw Fred Astaire and Cyd Charisse in *Silk Stockings* at the Southampton movie theater. Rivers kept laughing and saying that Fred Astaire looked dead. Then they went back to the house, where LeSueur wandered around and O'Hara and Rivers went to bed together.

O'Hara found the drug experience amusing but didn't seem eager to repeat it. He also didn't much like marijuana, but LeSueur recalled him pointing to a joint once and saying, "Let me have a drag off that. It might sober me up."

"And it did, too!" said LeSueur.

LeSueur praised O'Hara's gift for finding lovers all over New York City—including a night guard in the under-construction United Nations Building and a subway tollbooth attendant. Once, he said, a mailman came upstairs with a special-delivery letter, and O'Hara, dressed in short shorts, said, "You came all the way up here to deliver that? How about a beer?" The mailman patted O'Hara on the ass and said, "Very nice there." O'Hara said, "I'm hungover but I guess I wouldn't mind . . ."

This was before LeSueur moved in. Once he heard the story, he understood why sometimes the mailman would climb five flights of stairs just to deliver a regular letter.

LeSueur said O'Hara carried on this way until one night in 1956 when they hung out with W. H. Auden's partner Chester Kallman at the San Remo, a writer-friendly Greenwich Village bar.

> JL: We'd spent an evening sitting around drinking with Chester Kall-man. I don't know if you ever met him. He was a very excessive person, an opera buff, and had been a lover of Auden's and then they weren't lovers anymore. People assumed that was Frank and me, but it wasn't. We weren't lovers in the beginning. They'd become friends, lived on St. Marks Place, right where you are. He was given to telling stories about sexual adventures. They could be very funny. But on this particular night he was getting *very explicit*, bringing it down to a very vulgar level, talking about the size of the cock and all this stuff, and Wystan [W. H. Auden] calling to him: "Chester?" He would be sucking this guy's cock. "Yes, Wystan?" Really wild. But it was too much, I thought. It wasn't a moralistic thing. I liked Chester enormously, very bright and lively and funny.
>
> It would be 1956 because we took a cab downtown . . . it was before we moved downtown. We took a cab down Sixth Avenue [to the San Remo] and then uptown to Forty-Ninth Street. I sank back in that cab and said, "Frank, if you ever catch me talking that way— referring to Chester Kallman—take a gun, put it to my head, and shoot me. Don't ask me if I want to be shot. Just shoot me."
>
> About a year went by. By that time, we were living on University Place. I noticed that Frank wasn't doing wild things anymore. I was

certainly doing them if I got the chance. It's hard to be wild anymore because it's all too out in the open now. It ruined the scene—gay liberation, gay pride kind of thing—in a funny way. I said, "Frank, what's happened? Why aren't you carrying on anymore?"

He reminded me of that night, and he said, "I decided then that I wanted to do something else."

The "something else" was integrating sex into his friendships. LeSueur continued to compartmentalize: sex mostly with strangers; friends in another, platonic box. But O'Hara enjoyed the disarray that came from merging the two and from using the complications of love and sex as fodder for his poetry.

In a discussion of O'Hara's "Music" (1954), poet and critic Charles Simic said, "All lyric poems are narcissistic. They are the earliest form of personal ad. They've been saying for more than a thousand years, 'I'm a sensitive, vulnerable, misunderstood, barely solvent, loveable little fellow who would like to meet a person of exquisite taste who is not averse to an occasional roll in the hay.'"

My father tells LeSueur that O'Hara's sex-with-friends strategy is difficult for straight people, too: "In any circles, trying to get your sex and your friendship in the same place is murder! Are you kidding? I tried it for five years before I got married again, and I wouldn't have lasted another five. In terms of the emotional pressures, the jealousies."

These details about my father's 1970s sex life might be more than most people would want to know about their parents. And yet, I don't mind and I'm not shocked. Adults in the East Village always spoke bluntly about sex and drugs; those things were never taboo. Gallivanting, drinking, getting entangled—it all seems like the norm to me.

"We had nights," LeSueur said. "Frank liked to have an audience when he would do a number on me. There was a lot of sadism, but it was an act." In front of J. J. Mitchell and other friends, they would yell at each other until O'Hara, inevitably, got the last word.

And yet, they didn't go after each other where they were weak. LeSueur didn't feel smart. O'Hara felt unattractive, especially after his twenties. He didn't like his nose or his eyes, or his thinning hair. And so they reached a kind of truce, LeSueur said: "I attacked him on intellectual grounds, and he attacked me on physical grounds—where we were secure."

LeSueur said he thought O'Hara's rage came from being "an old soul" surrounded by oppressive forces. His mother, LeSueur said, was "a beautiful woman" but "a rotten person." He overheard O'Hara say to her on the phone more than once: "Why don't you go fuck yourself?"

According to LeSueur, those were his last words to her before he died, and her last words to him were: "Is that any way for a Harvard graduate to talk to his mother?"

There's a famous anecdote in which Jack Kerouac heckled Frank O'Hara. Drunk in the audience, he yelled: "You're killing American poetry, O'Harry!" O'Hara retorted: "That's more than you could do." But then LeSueur tells another Kerouac-O'Hara story, one I've never heard before.

> JL: Later at [artists' bar] the Cedar [Tavern], the same year, later that fall, they were both drunk and Kerouac was carrying on: "Here I thought you liked me, Frank!" Frank turned around and said, "I don't like you, Kerouac. It's your work I like!" And Kerouac *loved* that. From then on, they were very cozy, I think.

That sounds like my father. He's always been more comfortable being judged on the basis of his work than on his personality. I find that I like this version of O'Hara, even though he sounds a little mean.

It's a meanness born of intimacy and hyperattention, not estrangement and ignorance.

LeSueur moved out of his and O'Hara's Broadway apartment in 1965, but a couple of months before O'Hara died they had a last meal together at one of their usual spots. He thinks it was Sing Wu, around the corner from where I grew up, and my favorite restaurant when I was a kid.

Listening to this tape, I can taste the dumplings soaked in what my favorite waiter called Sam sauce. I'm sucked back into the past again, a tiny blond girl walking home with her parents after dinner.

Our East Village brownstone had no elevator. When people came over, they'd usually grow winded by the third floor, then they'd look up, realize they still had a long way to go, and mutter under their breath. My bedroom looked out over St. Marks Place, where drunks yelled curses and the M13 bus rattled down the street, shaking the windows.

Without close extended family, my parents and I were a tribe unto ourselves. Together we watched the seasons change through the skylights in the tar roof and beneath the translucent cover of the Entenmann's cupcake boxes on the kitchen counter: pink for Valentine's Day, green for St. Patrick's, plastic egg charms for Easter.

My father never bought me Christmas presents. He did not know my teachers, my friends, or my shoe size. That my father was in the picture was more than half my friends growing up in the 1980s could say. I saw him just about every day. He walked heavily on the wooden floors, got splinters like we all did, even when wearing thick socks.

To reach my father where he sat in his ash-blanketed office at the back of the apartment, I passed through our living room, then a dining room and kitchen, then another hallway, and past the bathroom. I would listen to hear if he was on the phone, the smell of cigarette smoke curling under the bottom of the door. If all was quiet, I would knock.

At 5:00 p.m. sharp, ice cubes *plink-plinked* into a glass, followed by Jack Daniels. Peter Jennings on TV, *60 Minutes*, *Jeopardy*. My mother, home after auditioning and running errands, would drink screw-drivers. There was always Rose's lime juice in the fridge, for the occasional gimlet.

"You were sick all the time," my father says when my childhood comes up. It's true. I had ear infections, bronchitis, strep throat. I missed weeks of school at a time and drank bottle after bottle of gooey pink antibiotics, swirled sometimes into my Dannon yogurt or chased with Tropicana orange juice. Looking back, I wonder if it may have had something to do with the fact that my parents smoked several packs a day between them and kept the windows closed.

I was also anxious. Music class, where we were expected to sing solos, gave me a stomachache. Upon learning what the middle finger meant, I became fearful that I would accidentally raise it at someone, so I sat on my hands. I declined to take a seat on the bus or subway for fear that I would not notice a pregnant or handicapped person who needed the seat more than I did. My parents joked about how I should be given "bad lessons."

In the 1980s, my mother stopped doing stand-up because her acting career took off. She played John Travolta's character's aunt in the movie *Urban Cowboy*. (Family legend has it I drank my first Coca-Cola at the famous honky-tonk Gilley's on Travolta's knee.) She appeared in character parts on *Family Ties* and *Murder, She Wrote* and was one of the stars of a short-lived sitcom called *Condo*, on which her husband was played by McLean Stevenson. She was making most of the money and working all the time, but she still found a way to clean the house and cook our meals. When she was away, my father heated up food she had made and left for us, or Stouffer's tuna noodle casserole, or Swanson Hungry-Man fried chicken.

My aunt Ann, who lived upstate, later said she worried about me in those days when my mother was away. She saw me as "a lost lamb." Starting in first grade, I traveled across town to and from school alone, watched several hours a day of TV in my room, and read books above my age level until I turned off my light.

On my walls, I wrote quotes—everything from Colette to La Rochefoucauld—in acrylic paint. I taped up postcards from my pen pals and posters of Ed Ruscha paintings. I strung Christmas lights and sat on the roof.

In one of my mother's efforts to have my father pay more attention to me, she sent him out to get me something. He came back from the Strand Bookstore with a stack of books, including W. H. Auden's *The Dyer's Hand* and Frank O'Hara's *Lunch Poems*.

I read the Auden book and liked it, but it went over my head. I was nine and hadn't yet developed a high tolerance for literary exegesis. *Lunch Poems*, though—that I loved right away. Whatever my father and I had in common that was good, I believed, was contained in that little orange-and-blue book from 1964. The Pocket Poets Series, number 19.

The poems seemed simple—they've been described as "I do this I do that" poems—but they had a substructure and a music to them. People who dismissed them as light or frothy were fools, I thought. The poems were simple like the Psalms are simple. The more times you repeat them, the more they reveal—not just the meaning of the words but the message of the sound. They were about TV and Coke, coffee and movie stars, and yet they felt like incantations.

My father had given me this book, which meant he wanted me to share in this thing he loved. He offered me so little of himself, but this gift was important and felt protective, like a talisman. I could carry it around in my backpack and read it on city buses and it could remind me that my father might not pay that much attention to me, but deep down, we understood each other. By loving his favorite writer, I could honor him the way other children might honor their father by joining his business.

From then on, I had O'Hara's poems in my head. That's thirty-five years of feeling possessed by him. When I finally saw him, in a PBS special, talking and walking and typing, I recognized his gait and his voice and his hands as if he were an old friend, even though I'd only ever seen pictures of him in books and never heard him speak. His friend, the poet Ron Padgett, called O'Hara's "a voice that often reminded me of bourbon and smoke, nightclubs, a phone call that changes your life, and warmth." To me, he sounded like New York, libraries, and my dad.

Chapter 3

The next tape I pick to play is marked "Barbara Guest." She was one of the New York School poets, but she's omitted from quite a few anthologies and chronicles of the group. I suspect it has something to do with the fact that fans of the genre appear to prefer the Beatles-esque symmetry of O'Hara, John Ashbery, James Schuyler, and Kenneth Koch, three of whom were gay and three of whom went to Harvard.

I like Guest right away. She's cheerful, open, trying to be helpful.

Barbara Guest—Water Mill, New York—8/17/77

Barbara Guest: I can see [Frank] now, going out from the museum, down the street and around the corner of Seventh Avenue—or Sixth, where they had the Picayunes. It was a very special thing. He didn't affect the French cigarettes the way Mike [Goldberg] did or others did, the Gauloises. It was the Picayunes.

The Internet tells me that Picayunes were a New Orleans regional tobacco brand sold in the South until the 1960s and "by far the strongest cigarettes ever made."

I have friends who are truly great reporters, who have won Pulitzer Prizes. I am not one of those people. And yet I have enough experience as a journalist to know that the follow-up question my father asks does not come from a place of confidence.

Peter Schjeldahl: Do you remember him always smoking them, or was it . . . ?

Guest pivots effortlessly, shares her own story. At age ten, she was sent to California from the South to live with her aunt and uncle in Beverly Hills. While a student at Berkeley, she went with other students from the college to visit Henry Miller at his home in the Pacific Palisades neighborhood of Los Angeles. She says Miller singled her out for attention—though she was neither protégé nor girlfriend, she insists. A Capricorn himself, Miller called her one of "those appalling Virgos" and told her she belonged in New York.

Guest took his advice. In New York, she says, many of the city's intellectuals had to "forgive" her for being Southern. But O'Hara was gentlemanly. He had what Guest told my father was "that quality of a thirties or forties movie: It's only you and the moonlight, you know?"

One day Guest wrote a poem while sitting at the fast-food restaurant Nedick's, and she knew that it was good. She placed it in *Commentary*, the intellectual magazine founded in 1945 by the American Jewish Committee. Another she sent to the *Partisan Review*. An editor there, the poet Delmore Schwartz, liked it and asked for more.

The painter Jane Freilicher saw Guest's poetry in the magazines and decided to look her up in the telephone book. Just like that, Guest had a new set of friends. She told my father about one winter night in the 1950s when she and O'Hara went to a party at a Greenwich Village studio. There were so many parties in those days—gangs of friends roamed from the Cedar Tavern to the San Remo to one downtown loft or uptown collector's apartment after another. After this party, O'Hara and Guest walked down Sixth Avenue.

> Barbara Guest: In those days, it seemed to snow more. We walked home in the snow and laughed and laughed and laughed. We rolled down the street in [the middle of] Sixth Avenue and threw snowballs at each other. Absolutely treating it as if it were a country town—and, furthermore, as Frank would have always pointed out, *our* town. You know, he always thought of New York as *his* town. Although neither one of us were New Yorkers.
> PS: Who is?
> BG: Well, some are. And they don't let you forget it.

As I listen to their voices emerge from the cassette player, I'm reminded that I'm here because O'Hara came to New York and made it *his* town. And that is what led my father to make it his—and mine and my family's.

My husband, Neal, born in the Piney Woods of East Texas, came to New York and began performing at theaters everywhere from holes-in-the-wall like Collective Unconscious on the Lower East Side to the Brooklyn Academy of Music. Our son, Oliver, rides the subway alone to and from his Times Square public school reading history books. He's been playing dress-up since infancy. We say his memoir would be titled *Where's My Helmet?* My stepson, Blake, age twenty-six, who grew up mostly in Texas with his mom, is studying for his doctorate in physical therapy at NYU, watching the sun set over Manhattan each evening from his sixteenth-floor window.

Together the four of us visit the Metropolitan Museum, the Museum of Natural History, Coney Island, Central Park. Alone, we each walk through neighborhoods, and we feel that the city is ours. Art world observer Martha King wrote: "Even casual acquaintances could feel [Frank O'Hara's] 'our' about New York City. He lived in the glamorous swirl the gifted lonely can invent in a great city."

The night after I listened to the Barbara Guest tape, my friend Jim took me to a concert at the Yotel. As I walked from the Eighth Avenue subway station, huge globs of wet snow snuck in around my flimsy umbrella and hit me in the face, and I thought of the Frank O'Hara line in his funniest poem, "Poem [Lana Turner has collapsed!]," in which it snows and rains in New York but not in Hollywood. I reminded myself this was not hail, because, as he says in that poem, hail is violent. This was just snow—wet, sneaky, aggressive snow, falling in soggy chunks on me and everyone else in Times Square.

Onstage, Jim's friend, Broadway star Tonya Pinkins, sang show tunes and gave a PowerPoint presentation on ancestry and the state of politics. It took Jim and me half an hour to get our first drinks, but we caught up and I had three glasses of wine.

When we left the building after congratulating Tonya, Jim and I saw that the snow had stopped. There is nothing quite like walking around New York City three-drinks drunk after a heavy snowfall. It feels like waking up, finally, to find that you're in the center of the universe. That is the feeling characters always have in Dawn Powell novels and in Replacements songs. You're alive. You're dead. You're both at once.

Chapter 4

When people say New York is bad now, I want to ask them: Compared with what? Places without a Met or a Cyclone or Ethiopian food? No, thank you. For all the changes, if you squint in the right part of town or at the right parties, you can still see the city O'Hara saw. I'm glad when I hear my father push back on the tapes whenever anyone says a word against New York or O'Hara's life here.

George Montgomery had a long life in the arts without ever becoming a household name. He had some poetry books published, got some exhibits as a photographer, served as director of the Museum of American Folk Art, and drank at the Cedar Tavern. In this interview, he functions as the classic college friend of the celebrity who insists the star has forgotten where he came from.

George Montgomery—SoHo, New York City (791 Broadway)—3/28/77
> George Montgomery: I just know we got on different paths. And even though we stayed close to each other because we'd been friends and still were, I didn't like the parties nor the people. I didn't like the fact that Frank didn't seem to be able to operate without an admirer. I

came to believe in myself as an anarchist, on my own. It disgusted me to see people want to talk with Frank about what they all talked about last night and to flatter him. Their whole lives became bound up in what they meant to him, or what they meant to others being that close to him. I came to hate the circle of people and to see it as a real danger. It wasn't that I wasn't in it. I came to loathe it as a way of life.

My father defends O'Hara's choices—maybe because they are his choices, too. He says that O'Hara and fellow New York School poets John Ashbery, Kenneth Koch, and James Schuyler made his life possible.

Peter Schjeldahl: What he and John Ashbery did, certainly, and then Kenneth to some extent, and then Jimmy Schuyler, and so on, was to create an option for a lifestyle for poetry that had not existed up to that time. At that point, the only lifestyle was university.

GM: I wonder if they created it or it simply happened and now it appears as though they did, like all of us when our lives—when someone else viewing it thinks that you've done it.

PS: Oh no! Not that they did it consciously.

GM: But that it is now possible for us because of the way they lived.

PS: I'm a poet. I dropped out of college. I came to New York. And I've made my living writing art criticism ever since, which was an option that was created by Frank and John. It didn't exist before.

My father tells Montgomery that he wound up with O'Hara's lifestyle and even with a descendant of his pets—a kitten named Basil born to O'Hara's cats Boris and Zelda.

Seeming determined to shock, Montgomery says that for O'Hara, part of being a poet was the sexual adventuring.

GM: I can remember a time when I brought home, believe it or not, two sailors. John [Ashbery] and Frank [O'Hara] were downstairs. The two sailors went downstairs to the bathroom, and they never came back. We always laughed about it because they both went off to John and Frank, and they never came back upstairs.

My father refused to be scandalized. While he's said that his own experimentation with homosexuality lasted just two weeks in the 1960s, he seems determined to defend O'Hara at all costs, even if that means hypothesizing a romantic encounter with him.

GM: Frank was very attracted to a married type.
PS: That's notorious.
GM: And to have a married man attracted to him really was wonderful, almost irresistible.
PS: As an old married man myself, I probably would have fallen for him if he had— [Laughs.]
GM: Yeah. And Frank was very, really unbelievably charming in actuality. You met him. He could really charm the birds from the trees. Maureen has a great deal of it. Maybe it's just in knowing Frank, but when I speak to Maureen, I can hear Frank talking. I don't know. There's a kind of Irish hyperbole or something. There's a kind of a lilt, a charm to the language.
PS: I have great trouble with Maureen.
GM: Really?
PS: Yeah. She chose me to write the book and since then . . . I'll turn off the tape recorder. [*Click.*]

While I still believe I'll have better luck with Maureen than my father did, I'm beginning to worry a little. As I start reading books about O'Hara and asking people about him, I keep noticing ways in which his work is less available than you'd think it might be given his stature. O'Hara's poetry is not available in eBook, for example.

And I keep hearing stories about projects for which she's withheld permissions—including, most surprisingly to me, a picture book about Frank O'Hara by a respected children's book author.

In her academic book *Frank O'Hara: Poet Among Painters*, published in 1977 and dedicated to Maureen Granville-Smith, Marjorie Perloff wrote that O'Hara's friends persuaded her "that the time is not yet ripe for a biography, because their versions of specific incidents did not always coincide."

Next to this line in my father's copy, he'd written a large exclamation point. I mentally added my own. *Why would the time be ripe later? How would their versions of events grow together? What was everyone so scared of?*

The largest void in O'Hara scholarship are his letters, which have never been collected. I'd heard that my father's friend Ron Padgett, who lived just five blocks from us on St. Marks Place, at one time was given the job of editing a volume of O'Hara's letters. I emailed him to invite myself over.

Walking toward Ron Padgett's East Village apartment one winter afternoon, I think of this piece of his "Poem" (1980):

> Funny, I hear
> Frank O'Hara's
> voice tonight
> in my head—
> e.g. when I
> think in words
> he's saying them
> or his tone
> is in them.

Ron greets me at the door of his apartment wearing brown corduroy pants and white sneakers. Frank O'Hara is still one of his favorite poets: "He seemed to be giving us permission to do a lot of things artistically. Also, there was just this magic to him. That's a bad word, I know, but some of his poems actually have this magic to them. I read them and I still can't quite puzzle some of them out and yet they affect me."

He saw O'Hara a number of times and each time found that there was something about him that set people at ease. Given that the scene could be competitive, this warmth was especially disarming: "He made it seem okay to like other people."

In Manhattan, Padgett wound up at parties with O'Hara and other writers he'd admired as a teenager in Tulsa. One night, he and his wife, Pat, and his teacher Kenneth Koch and Koch's wife, Janice, went to dinner at O'Hara's loft on Broadway and Eleventh Street when O'Hara was still living there with Joe LeSueur. Pat and Ron were buzzed in and climbed the industrial stairs until they arrived, slightly winded, at the landing. Ron looked down the hallway, and Frank was standing there with the door propped open. O'Hara said, "I'm so glad you could come tonight."

Padgett said, "Oh, thank you for inviting us."

Then O'Hara said, "I like your poetry."

Flummoxed, Padgett blurted out: "I like yours, too!"

O'Hara cracked up because of the awkwardness. "But he cracked up in a nice way that made me feel good and not in a way that made me feel like a fool."

The apartment itself "was pretty magnificent," Padgett said. "It had white walls. The bricks were painted white. I remember an orange butterfly chair. He had a de Kooning and a Jean Dubuffet. It was spacious. It was cool. Joe LeSueur made his famous chili that night, which is one of my favorite dishes. It wasn't that easy to get in New York back in the sixties."

After dinner they were sitting on the couches and once again O'Hara set Padgett at ease.

Ron Padgett—East Village, New York City—2/7/19

Ron Padgett: I found myself talking to Joe LeSueur, and Frank and Kenneth fell into this very animated conversation. I was kind of half listening to Joe LeSueur, half trying to catch what they were saying. Anyway, at a certain point in the evening, Frank sort of shifted his attention to me, and he said something like— I don't know how we got on to the subject of Jean Genet. I had read a number of Genet's books by that time. This would have been about 1964 or so. Maybe I was still a senior at Columbia. Frank said something like, when I said, "Jean Genet," he said, "Oh! What have you been reading of Genet?" And I suddenly went blank. I couldn't remember the title. I think it was *Our Lady of the Flowers*, but I'm not sure. I went totally blank, and I looked at him and I said, "Oh, I don't know. I just read books just so they'll make me write." He gave me this great chuckle and warm smile and said, "Yeah, it's all just grist for the mill, isn't it?" And that was a very sweet thing to get me out of an awkward moment, I thought. That was typical of the way he treated me, always.

A contemporary of my father's, Padgett grew up in Oklahoma, the son of a bootlegger. Aside from the occasional cowboy novel or *Field and Stream* magazine, there wasn't a lot to read in his house, but his middle school English teacher taught him how to diagram sentences and made him keep a reading chart that he still has. It starts with *Hot Rod* magazine and ends with Shakespeare. By then he was haunting Tulsa's public library, and he got a job at the bookshop, where the owner one day asked a fateful question of Padgett, who was sixteen, and his friend, the poet Dick Gallup, who was seventeen: "Have you boys read Kerouac?"

Padgett started reading *Evergreen Review* and everything from Grove Press and City Lights. He decided that he and Gallup and Joe Brainard should start their own magazine, so they wrote to their heroes asking for submissions and got a 90 percent response rate. Between 1958 and 1960, they published five issues of the *White Dove Review*. A neighbor named Ted Berrigan (who later moved to 101 St. Marks Place, a block from my parents) started shoving poems into their money box at the bookstore.

As soon as they could, Padgett and Brainard moved to New York. Padgett started studying at Columbia with Kenneth Koch, and there he was, bam, a member—along with his friends Berrigan, Gallup, Brainard, and my father—of the second generation of what he referred to as "the so-called-so-called New York School" because its members were self-conscious from the jump.

The last time Padgett saw O'Hara, O'Hara wasn't wearing pants. As Padgett was about to leave a party, he headed to the bedroom, where guests' coats were piled on the bed. He passed painter John Button and author Christopher Isherwood (whose book *Berlin Stories* inspired the musical *Cabaret*, then soon to debut on Broadway) and opened the bedroom door.

RP: I went into the bedroom. I walked in and looked across the room and there was Joe LeSueur and there was Frank, who was just putting on his pants. But there was nothing erotic about it. Nothing had happened. Frank was actually just changing clothes because he had to go to a fancier party uptown, like a MoMA event or something. He was putting on a serious suit and tie kind of thing. He was just pulling his pants up. Just as I walked in, Frank had his pants about at his knees and he looked over at me and he looked at Joe and said, "Oh, what's he going to think of us now?" Which struck me as so funny. That was typical, again, of the wit, but also relieving me of my embarrassment.

* * *

Padgett met my father through the poetry scene in 1962. Padgett's first impression of him was that he wasn't a rich kid, exactly, but that he seemed to have a safety net that not a lot of poets his age did. "I didn't know anybody else in New York who had a sports car," Padgett said.

While attending Carleton College in Northfield, Minnesota, my father had begun publishing an offset-printed poetry magazine called *Mother*. He did such a good job pretending *Mother* was a legitimate enterprise that he was able to solicit work from some of the star poets of the day and to strike up friendships with some of them. He even wrote, in his hero's honor, a poem titled "After Frank O'Hara" and got one of his new friends to show it to O'Hara.

O'Hara responded: "Oh no! Someone's after me!" He also said he liked the poem.

Hoping for a job, my father sent resumes to newspapers all over the country. The only one that invited him in for an interview was the *Jersey Journal*, so he packed up his books and drove the aforementioned sports car, a new yellow Austin-Healey Sprite, a convertible two-seat roadster his parents bought for him, to Jersey City. On regular trips into Manhattan, he attended poetry readings and took Koch's classes at the New School.

In 1963, my father went back to Carleton for his junior year but soon dropped out for good and returned to New York with a college girlfriend, Linda O'Brien. They married at city hall and, after a year as expatriates in Paris, took a tenement apartment on Avenue B.

My father and Ron Padgett became good friends. In 1968, they gave a reading together at the painter Red Grooms's loft to coincide with the publication of an anthology called *The Young American Poets*, edited by Paul Carroll.

"Peter and I cooked up this plan that I think worked wonderfully, without telling anyone in the audience, although a lot of the people were friends of ours and could figure it out, but the unsuspecting wouldn't know. We read each other's poetry without saying so: 'Here's a new poem,' and then I would read a thing by Peter. Funny thing was, I liked your father's work, obviously, but that day I gained a new respect for his work by reading it as if I were he. That was so much fun. He and I both felt a mischievous glee at doing it."

We talked about my doing this project, and Padgett told me about writing a biography of his father, the bootlegger. He found it very difficult: "I couldn't get my head around who my father was. I couldn't quite deal with the power of his personality. I don't mean he was oppressive or awful or anything. Not at all. All in all, he treated me quite well. I just thought, *I've got to do justice to the person he was without lying.*"

Toward the end of our time together I get around to asking about why the collection of O'Hara letters he was editing never came out. His eyes flash and his lips purse. This is so unlike him that I am taken aback. All Padgett will say is that he and Maureen came to a disagreement that caused the project to be canceled.

As I continue to pull every book about Frank O'Hara that the New York Public Library has to offer, I realize that, to date, the only one who has come close to substantially collecting the O'Hara letters is a CUNY graduate student and Legacy Fieldwork Fellow named Josh Schneiderman. His two chapbooks contain sixteen effusive letters exchanged between Kenneth Koch and Frank O'Hara in 1955–56.

I decide to invite Schneiderman out for a drink and to ask him how Maureen might like to be approached. It's the kind of thing my father would never think to do. And thinking of things like that is why I am sure to succeed where he failed.

Chapter 5

When I walked into Sugarburg, a bar near my Brooklyn apartment, I was startled to discover that the Legacy Fieldwork Fellow was distractingly handsome. I was possessed by a sudden conspiracy theory as I mentally lined up all the good-looking men who had been given permission for O'Hara's material. Brad Gooch was literally a fashion model, and this guy could've been January in a fireman calendar. Then I thought, *No, there were also a couple of women*. But I liked the idea that the estate might have shown a partiality to heartthrobs, just as O'Hara had swooned over movie star Tab Hunter.

Josh Schneiderman, a tattooed grad student from Philly teaching writing and American literature at Hunter, told me he thought he knew why I was there. I was glad, because looking at his muscled forearms I had forgotten. Everybody wanted to know how he'd convinced Maureen to give him permission to reprint some of her brother's letters.

As I copied him in ordering a whiskey and treated us to bar snacks, he told me about his girlfriend, his dog, and how much he loved the New York School. His advice about Maureen was this: be very clear with her about what you're doing and be patient. It might have been the whiskey, but I felt empowered leaving that bar.

The next day, I wrote Maureen an email with the subject "journalist inquiry," explaining what I'd like to do and telling the Barbara Guest story about the snowball fight. I explained that I'd found the tapes and learned that my father had never finished his O'Hara book and that I wanted to make it right. I said that I'd love to come to Connecticut to interview her at her convenience and to tell her more about the proposed project.

A few days later, I was over at my parents' apartment on St. Marks Place for dinner. I told them about Josh and how having his advice would surely help. I asked my father if he still had the Nakian catalog that O'Hara inscribed to him. He reached into the bookshelf and handed it to me, said I could keep it. The book had teeth marks along the spine, a victim of my childhood pet rabbit. For years, lop-eared, litter-trained Ginger hopped around the apartment and gnawed everything within reach—art catalogs, Broadway cast recordings, a rare Lynda Benglis sculpture. One day, he bit into a wire and was electrocuted.

According to my father, there was at least one other would-be biographer between him and Brad Gooch: the art writer and documentary filmmaker Amei Wallach, who was working on her O'Hara biography in the 1980s when permission to quote from O'Hara's poetry was rescinded. He said he would email her for me because he had given her some of his research back then and he thought maybe it would be useful to me.

Then, to all of us but really to Oliver, my father read "The Day Lady Died," "Poem [Lana Turner has collapsed!]," and Kenneth Koch's poem in imitation of Robert Frost, the one with the verse "for hay is dried-up grass / When you're alone."

Oliver burst out laughing, just like I had the first time I'd heard it.

My father remarked on the serendipity that had brought him—and so all of us—to New York.

Born in 1942, he was the first child of a young middle-class Norwegian-Lutheran couple in Fargo, North Dakota. His mother, Charlene, had gone to school for journalism. She'd always wanted to be a writer but instead she became a housewife and helpmeet to her husband, G. T., whom everyone called a genius. When G. T. returned from World War II, he became an entrepreneur with his own company. The couple had one more boy, Don, and three girls, Ann, Peggy, and Mary.

My grandfather was most famous as the inventor of the airsickness bag and the fabricator of material used in Echo 1, the first communications satellite. He was obsessive about his work and tended to notice his children only when they were doing something that interested him personally. He didn't like to stop the car on road trips, even to see the sights. On one trip, in his eagerness to get back on the road, he inadvertently left two of his young children, Peggy and Don, at a gas station. When he returned, after eventually noticing the back seat was quieter than usual, their faces were covered in tears and snot—and ice cream that had been given to them by a good Samaritan.

My father never got along with his father. He found both his parents cold and self-involved. And he bridled at the pressure to be a good role model for his four younger siblings. As a hypersensitive boy in the Midwest, he knew his real life was somewhere else.

At the age of twenty-one, my father came across Frank O'Hara in an anthology edited by Donald Allen: *New American Poetry 1945–1960*. Allen's book made contemporary poetry seem urgent. Its greatest revelation for my father was Frank O'Hara's New York City: jovial drunkenness, Times Square billboards, Greenwich Village parties that spilled out into the street.

After giving up on ever graduating from college, my father moved to New York for good to be a part of the poetry world. Once there, he attended parties with guest lists that mimicked the Donald Allen anthology contributors' page: Kenneth Koch in his big glasses and messy hair. Ron Padgett in his big glasses and messy hair. And, burning brighter than anyone else, Frank O'Hara. My father wanted to be a part of O'Hara's world. And, with effort and talent, he succeeded.

Sitting in his East Village apartment, my father told a version of this story that he'd told many times before, and he concluded it with the happy ending: "And now here we all are!"

I sank into the couch with the cocktail my mother had made me and looked around in astonishment: How lucky I was. There was no better place to grow up than this. Even if I liked our Midwestern extended family much more than he did, I had to admit that he'd been right to start his family here. This was the promised land.

And now I was going to finish what he'd started as a young man back in the Midwest with his "After Frank O'Hara" poem. I was taking over the pursuit of our hero, and I was going to catch him at last because I was going to get Maureen to talk to me. I was going to bring those tapes out of the basement and into the light. Marcel Proust wrote: "To write that essential book, which is the only true one, a great writer does not, in the current meaning of the word, invent it, but, since it exists already in each one of us, interprets it."

That's how this book began to seem: like I didn't even have to go out of my way for it; it was coming to me.

Chapter 6

Invigorated, the next day at the library I put my headphones on and listened to an interview with Larry Osgood, one of O'Hara's Harvard friends and a novelist then living in SoHo. After World War II, Osgood had arrived at Harvard from Buffalo, New York, to find a campus teeming with veterans taking advantage of the G.I. Bill. It was the first time he'd ever been away from home. As a roommate of one of O'Hara's friends at Eliot House, he fell in with the intellectual gang including O'Hara, Lyon Phelps, George Montgomery, Hal Fondren, Edward Gorey, Freddy English, and Violet R. "Bunny" Lang. Of the group, Osgood was the youngest and least sophisticated. "My eyes were opened very wide, and my ears were open very wide," he said. "I didn't have very much to say."

As Osgood and my father talked in Osgood's apartment on Wooster Street, there was street noise in the background, and a cat meowed into the recorder. My father seemed stressed out. When presented with Osgood's letters from O'Hara, my father said there was no need to look at them because he would be receiving the lot any day from Maureen.

You sure about that? I almost say out loud.

Then Osgood described how he and O'Hara became lovers.

Larry Osgood—SoHo, New York City (141 Wooster Street)—6/1/77

Larry Osgood: We were standing around on a street corner. This must
   have been in January or February of 1950. We were trying to decide
   if we should go to the Harvard liquor store and buy a pint of rye and
   go back to Frank's apartment and drink or whether we should—

Peter Schjeldahl: The liquor store was open after midnight?

LO: Yes, it was. Maybe it closed at midnight, but there was always a
   period before last call at [the popular student bar] Cronin's and the
   time the liquor store closed. We were trying to decide whether we
   should do that or not and Frank finally turned to me and said, "Well,
   it's about time *you* decided something, Larry." So I said, "Well, okay,
   let's buy a pint of liquor and go back to your apartment." We all got
   drunk at Frank's place . . . We got to dancing with each other. And I
   spent the night with Frank that night. And fell just hopelessly in love
   with Frank O'Hara. And for the rest of the spring we had an affair
   going . . . I was very serious about the affair myself. And I think Frank
   didn't want that particularly. As I look back on it, I realize that I rather
   instinctively pulled every possible trick a lover can pull to keep a lover,
   without really intending to do so, without calculatingly doing it.

Osgood still sounded a little bit lovesick, in that way one often
is when it's not clear what an affair meant to the other person. He
recalled a code they had: If O'Hara said, "Would you like to come up
and listen to Schumann?" it meant "Would you like to spend the night
with me?" Osgood mused about whether O'Hara had ever slept with
their other friend, George Montgomery.

My father, seemingly oblivious to how sensitive Osgood was on
this score and eager to show off that he had been doing his research,

told Osgood that O'Hara and Montgomery had indeed been lovers. I winced when he said it, sure that Osgood would have preferred to live with the mystery.

There was a push-pull between Osgood and O'Hara for years. Osgood decided that O'Hara had a psychological block against ever getting too close to anyone—that time-honored refuge of the scorned.

LO: Maybe half a dozen—no, maybe not that many. Say, on three or four occasions Frank would have very black depressions. I don't know what the source of them was, but he would literally draw the blinds and lie on the couch all day or most of the day and simply not want to be disturbed by anybody at all. I don't know what it was that he was going through, but that did happen from time to time that spring when I knew him.

PS: Compensating for manic [episode]s?

LO: It's so hard to say if Frank was ever manic because it seemed like he was manic much of the time. Frank's energy was always . . .

PS: He certainly seemed remarkably free of neurosis.

LO: Hmm.

PS: He was one of the few members of his generation who was never in psychoanalysis. Do you remember him talking about psychoanalysis?

LO: I would certainly talk to him about mine. I had what I suppose was a mini analysis with Frank during that spring because a lot of the times we were alone together were spent with me talking to him and telling him about my problems and Frank's elucidating things for me.

PS: What was his theoretical framework?

LO: Mostly that the way to deal with problems of that nature, psycho-logical problems in general, was to do something. It was an activist attitude. With the exception of the times he lay on the couch for three hours without stirring, it was to write a poem. To read a book. To take a walk. To call up somebody.

PS: To have an affair.

LO: Have an affair. Have drinks. Have a conversation. This is a little colored by a conversation I had with Joe LeSueur a few days ago or a couple of weeks ago about Jimmy Schuyler, and when Jimmy started having psychological problems and started having his first breakdown while he was living with Frank. And how Frank wanted *nothing* to do with it. Really even in a somewhat ruthless way. Frank could be a very ruthless person. He just didn't want to see that or look at it or deal with it or become part of it.

PS: Could it have been a realistic admission of his own inability? He didn't have much appetite for lost causes.

LO: None at all. I think with me that spring of 1950 he was extremely gentle on a lot of occasions and very mean and bitchy on others. I think anyone who ever was in love with Frank experienced that absolutely unexpected streak of close to viciousness in Frank. That would come out in retrospect. Perhaps it would happen if he was touched too close and felt that the other person at that moment was going to interfere with—was going to reach him in a way he didn't want to be reached—that would interfere with his work and fuck him up. Frank from the very beginning—one of the extraordinary things from the very beginning—was so completely a poet that that really governed his life. As I was just actually writing to Don Allen about the early writings, Frank's voice is altogether there. It became richer and fuller, and the poems got a lot better. But even then he had made up his mind and had become a poet. Period.

I'm reminded of what another friend of O'Hara's, Kenward Elmslie, said: "He didn't set a value judgment on emotions. That's what gets you into analysis. Panic is what happens. And he evidently never panicked. Or if he did, he would accept the panic. Then he was in a panic. Then he was in a rage. Then he was wildly aroused. He accepted each shift as it came."

I imagine my father, forever consumed with panic, listening to this description of a man truly okay with who he was. I wonder why he tried to emulate his hero in so many ways, but not in this one.

Chapter 7

In the middle of the stack of tapes, I notice a couple with my name on them. I am a little afraid but also deeply curious. When I hit Play, I hear myself.

Ada—New York City—9/77

Ada: What's that?

Peter Schjeldahl: It's a tape recorder.

A: Yeah.

PS: Yeah. Tape recorder. It's a button. Daddy's. Daddy's.

A: Daddy's!

PS: Yes. Daddy's tape recorder. You can't have it because it's Daddy's.

A: Dad-dy.

PS: Uh-huh. Isn't it nice? Isn't that nice? Huh?

A: [Fussing.]

PS: [Sound of exasperation.]

On that tape, I'm a year and a half old. On another, I'm two and a half. My father and I sing:

Ada's Bedtime—New York City—11/22/78

PS and A: *Daisy, daisy, give me your answer do . . .*
I'm half-crazy all for the love of you.
It won't be a stylish marriage
I can't afford a carriage
But you'll look neat
Upon the seat
Of a bicycle built for two.

It's strange to hear my parents—whom I've known only as middle-aged or old people—as new parents in their thirties and to hear myself reciting nursery rhymes for them.

A: *Jack and Jill went up the hill*
   to fetch a pail of water.
   Jack fell down and broke his crown
   and Jill came tumbling after.
Brooke Alderson: What about Humpty Dumpty?
A: *Humpty Dumpty sat on a wall.*
   Humpty Dumpty had a great fall.
   All the king's horses and all the king's men
   couldn't put Humpty Dumpty back together again.
BA: Terrific!

I rattle off "Wee Willie Winkie" and "Peter Peter Pumpkin Eater" and "Hey Diddle Diddle" and "Jack Be Nimble" and "Jack Sprat": But betwixt the two of them, they licked the platter clean.

It's bizarre to hear my voice. It's also exhilarating. I mean, I was still in diapers, and I knew the word "betwixt." I was a *genius!*

In my toddler voice, I ask my father to play the tape back. He thinks I'm saying there are people in the tape recorder. He says there are no people living in the tape recorder.

In my baby voice I say I know that. I just want them to play the tape back.

From the vantage point of forty years later, having babysat countless children and raised my own verbose child, I can hear the frustration in my baby voice.

BA: There are not people in there! Ready? Let's sing into it. Then we'll play it back. Okay? It just tapes our voices.

A: When we play it back, Dad do it?

BA: [Mishearing my "we."] *They* won't do it!

PS: [From elsewhere in the room.] It's a *machine*, Ada!

BA: It's a machine. There aren't people in there.

I think, not for the first time, that these are not people to whom parenting came naturally. Once I asked them how they decided to have a child in the first place.

"We thought your mother was pregnant and we thought, 'Oh no! Not a kid! That will ruin everything!'" my father said. "But then it turned out she wasn't pregnant, and we were sad about it. So we decided to have one on purpose."

My mother disputes this and says they always wanted a baby.

They do agree that when she found out she was pregnant with me, they threw a big dinner party. While I was growing up, famous artists of the era huffed up those stairs to eat dinner around our table: Ed Ruscha, Bruce Nauman, Cindy Sherman, David Salle, Eric Fischl. At this one dinner they solicited advice on baby names. With the last name Schjeldahl, they wanted something as easy as possible for the first name. Jane? Daisy?

Ada Katz, known as "the most painted woman of the twentieth century" because her husband, Alex, made so many portraits of her, said, "I've always thought Ada was a nice name."

So it was settled.

What strikes me most on these tapes I appear on is how charmed and surprised my parents seem to be by this small person in their midst. They had never known babies before. Neither had my mother's friends, most of whom were gay men. She and her accompanist and best friend, Gary Simmons, called me the Christ Child. I had colic, which meant I was fussy for the first six months, but once that cleared up it was generally agreed that I was bright, kind, and quiet—no trouble, even in my frequent sickness.

Author Christopher Isherwood, in his diaries, recalled meeting me at a party at his home. He said: "One of the most agreeable children imaginable, neither sulky nor sly nor pushy nor ugly, with a charming trustful smile for all of us, she went off without the slightest protest and slept in our bed until it was time for everybody to leave."

When I was three, my parents and some friends went on a hike through the desert in California. My mom recalls that they kept yelling at me, "Keep up, Ada!" And then she realized, at the end of a long, hot day, that I'd done all those miles of hiking on legs that were a third the size of theirs. *And, can you believe it? Covered in sunburn and sweat, she didn't complain once!* A lot of stories about me as a little girl were like this—how independent, how uncomplaining, how good.

My father never did know how to relate to me. He tried some things that made sense and some that did not. When I was in kindergarten, he typed up a bedtime story about a stuffed animal called Doctor Bear. The same year, he showed me *Judgment at Nuremberg*. I was so traumatized by the movie's graphic concentration camp scenes that soon after, when I saw a Hasidic man walking down the street, I shrieked and said, "Oh no! Will he be okay?"

My father showed me how to look up big words in his huge dictionary, how to keep a baseball box score, and how to throw a punch, which he encouraged me to do if I was bothered by the older playground bully. When I was in first grade, he taught me how to touch-type on his IBM Selectric, my brow furrowed and my tiny fingers searching for the letters without looking down.

And from elementary school on, every time I was at the base of Central Park and saw the bronze Augustus Saint-Gaudens statue of General Sherman, I would think of a line in O'Hara's poem "Music." When he looks at the statue, he sees the angel leading Sherman's horse into Bergdorf's. I never would have thought of that if my father hadn't given me *Lunch Poems*.

But I'm getting distracted. I need to get back to the tapes. I need to focus on Frank O'Hara and stop thinking about my own childhood. I pick a tape that I think will be good: Hal Fondren. I soon learn that Fondren, who shows up often in O'Hara's poetry, was a gay air force veteran from Kentucky with whom O'Hara threw regular cocktail parties at Harvard.

Hal Fondren—12/19/77

Hal Fondren: You had ten dollars and you bought two bottles of gin or three bottles of gin and a bottle of vermouth and offered everyone martinis. They went quite a long way because we knew a lot of freshmen, and a lot of the boys brought freshman girls who'd never drunk a martini in their lives.

Peter Schjeldahl: It went a long way.

HF: It went a long way. There was usually enough for me and Frank to get *really loaded*.

They usually had enough Cinzano vermouth left over to have an aperitif before lunch the following day. The sounds of ice tumbling into glasses and lighters flicking on—and the very relaxed tone of Fondren's voice—make me think he and my father were drinking and smoking throughout this interview.

It makes me wonder how my father felt interviewing all these war veterans. He told me many times that when he was called up for Vietnam, he'd taken every drug he could get his hands on and then showed up to the draft board and tried to cooperate. They threw him out like he was trash. And, unfortunately, he played the part of a deranged addict too well. It took him a while to feel normal again after that performance.

In any case, it doesn't come up, and the interview goes somewhere none of the others have. Hal Fondren may have been the only Harvard friend from that time whom O'Hara took home with him for a visit.

HF: It was a very strange experience, actually.
PS: Tell me all you can remember about it. [Clock chimes. Fondren laughs.] I've yet to make contact with the family and childhood friends, and he rarely talked about it.

I'm riveted. I can't believe I'm actually going to get to follow Fondren home with O'Hara to Grafton. I turn the volume up and push my headphones closer to my head.

The trip began auspiciously enough. O'Hara picked Fondren up from the train and took him out to a series of bars on the way back to the house. They couldn't drink at home and so they'd better do it on the way there, O'Hara said. Their new discovery was India pale ale, so they drank a few of those.

When they arrived home, they sat with Maureen, then a young girl, and had a lovely dinner made by O'Hara's mother, Kay, whom Fondren found lively and attractive. After scarfing it down, O'Hara announced that they had to leave again to go see some friends in a show at the Red Barn Theater. When the show got out, O'Hara said he was leaving with a girl but that he'd meet back up with Fondren at the Grafton town square a couple of hours later. Fondren was dropped off by a couple of people at the square on time, but O'Hara never arrived. It began to rain. Fortunately, Fondren had a good sense of direction, so he figured out the way back to the O'Hara home.

HF: I found his house, which was dark and completely locked up. All the doors were locked. The garage door was shut, and I could see that the car was in the garage. I even tried a couple of windows, but everything was locked. And then presently a light went on. Someone obviously heard me trying to break in. It was Frank's mother.

She said, "Hal? Hal, is that you?"

I said, "Yes!"

She already had the coffee pot plugged in and was prepared to have a long discussion.

She said, "What on earth happened?"

I said, "Well, I don't know what you mean. Frank took this girl home after the play, and I got a ride with a couple of his friends who brought me back to Grafton."

She said, "Who?"

Well, that was sort of a sticker. Of course it wasn't a friend of Frank's at all who brought me back to Grafton. And I said, "Well, I can't really remember their names, but it's beside the point . . . What happened to Frank? Did he get home?"

She said, "Well, he's very drunk, and the car's all smashed up."

I could only see the back end of it through the garage door. It looked perfectly all right to me, but as it happened the front fender was caved in a little. She poured us out some black coffee and she said, "Are you boys drinking a great deal at Harvard?"

I said, "Well, I don't know. I don't think we drink any more than usual. We usually just drink beer except when we have one of our famous cocktail parties, where we drink martinis. Ordinarily we can't afford anything but beer and you can't go very far on that."

At daybreak the next morning, O'Hara went into Fondren's room looking like death and said, "I can't remember how I got home." Fondren said, "It was all that India pale ale." O'Hara had chased the IPAs with a number of cocktails. That was the only significant interaction Fondren remembered having with O'Hara's family until graduation day in 1950, when the drunk one was O'Hara's mother.

HF: She had a couple of drinks. That's why I know that Frank had never mentioned her having a drinking problem at all.
PS: Did it make for a noticeable change in her behavior?
HF: Yes, it did, and it was all very unfortunate. So we somehow got through this dismal lunch.
PS: How did she behave? [Sound of children playing outside. Long pause.]
HF: I can't remember exactly. She just seemed to get awfully drunk and started talking about personal family history in a way that I don't think she would have—
PS: Maudlin, abusive?
HF: Yes.
PS: All of that?
HF: All of that. She was very maudlin. And she kept picking on Frank. And, well, it wasn't very entertaining for anyone else.
PS: Accusing him of not—
HF: Well, of not paying any attention to her and never coming home. [Clock chimes.] The usual mother's tirade.

PS: And how did Frank take it?

HF: Frank was just embarrassed. He kept saying, "Oh, shut up, Mother," which didn't have much effect. I'm rather vague about it now because I heard so much about this later when we lived together in New York.

My father taught at Harvard for a little while. When it came time for me to go to college, I attended McGill in Montreal and the University of Texas at Austin, two schools that gave me nearly full scholarships. I received a fine education at both. Life in Austin was fun and easy compared to life in New York. I drove a little Ford Escort, ate breakfast tacos, studied Sanskrit, paid almost nothing in rent, and got a work-study job cataloguing the D. H. Lawrence collection at the Harry Ransom Center archive.

I dropped my father's surname and started using my middle name, Calhoun, as my last. The second I did it, I felt like I could write without bearing the burden of my father's name, and I became a frequent contributor to the *Austin Chronicle*. I liked UT. But in exchange for graduating with barely any debt, I failed to develop an Ivy Leaguer's never-been-punched-in-the-face swagger.

My father asked me to cook for the Harvard kids when they visited, and he held court with them at the dinner table while I cleaned up. One summer when I returned from college to the St. Marks apartment for a couple of weeks, I discovered that my father had given my bedroom to Matt, one of his Harvard TAs, for weeks as a bedroom and art studio. Matt had thoughtfully taped tarps over my closet. I let Matt keep my room, and I slept on the couch. He and I eventually became friends, but he was the only one from that group that I could tolerate.

Once at a gathering in my parents' living room, one of them approached me in between my serving duties and asked what I was reading.

I suspected he was only asking so he'd have a prompt to show off what *he* was reading.

"*Encyclopedia Brown*," I said, correctly sensing that the mention of a children's book series about a boy detective would stun him long enough so I could get away.

For twenty-six years, until just a few years ago, my parents would throw a massive Fourth of July party in the Catskills. My father said that everyone who heard of it was invited. The fireworks display was phenomenal. He enlisted a crew of friends to help him set it off. Together they lit up the mountain. Tents with potluck food filled the gardens. After the fireworks show, there was a bonfire by the pond.

At one of these fireworks shows, Neal was struck in the neck by a firework and for a year had a burn scar shaped like the Philippines. Another year, our friend was shot with one while holding his one-year-old. The baby was fine, if scared, but our friend's arm was burned. At yet another party, when the bonfire was lit, fireworks shot out from it in all directions, causing parents to dive to the ground, pushing their children into the grass to keep them from getting hit.

"Unbelievable! What idiots did this?" my mother yelled, collaring teenagers. My father was conspicuously silent. We later learned that he was the one who'd hidden the fireworks in the bonfire, as a fun surprise.

"You know what your motto is?" I told my father. "Safety third."

At the final party an ambulance had to be called for a man having a heart attack and two children almost drowned in the pond, two thousand people attended. The line to the five porta potties stretched all the way down the driveway.

A few years before, I'd walked into my room hours before the party to find a random stranger changing into her bathing suit; she acted like I was in her way. Once attendance passed a thousand, the house became too chaotic a place to put a little kid down for a nap, so for the weekend we rented a room at the nearby inn that was now run by my mother's best friend and former accompanist, my honorary uncle Gary. When I told my father the plan, his response was to disinvite us. He said, "You obviously hate the party, so you shouldn't come."

For years, he'd invited everyone he knew to the party—his Harvard students, his colleagues at the *New Yorker*, all his oldest and newest friends. He even put an invite to the party in a published essay so that all his readers would know they could go, too. I was enraged that everyone who'd ever heard of the party was invited but that year I was not.

Chapter 8

When I picked up my ringing phone one afternoon as I made a post-school snack for Oliver, I saw that the caller was Josh, the CUNY grad student who had published the chapbooks of O'Hara letters. I left Oliver in the living room to take the call and closed the bedroom door behind me.

"So, Maureen called me yesterday," Josh began. "I'm guessing she hasn't called you, right?"

She had not. He said she'd thanked him for putting us in touch and wanted to ask him if I was on the level. "She said that she would talk to you and that she would be interested in meeting. She didn't say when, but that's kind of the way things go with her. She said that she sees no reason why the interviews shouldn't be published, which I know isn't the whole deal but it's a step that seems positive."

Then he said that Maureen told him that what turned her off of my father doing his project was one time when he came to see her along with my mother and me when I was a baby.

I asked Josh if Maureen told him what my father said.

"Yeah, it's kind of funny actually," he said. "She said that when he came to visit, he denigrated O'Hara in comparison with Ashbery:

'Well, you know, Ashbery was the better critic and the better poet, but Frank was a more important figure socially.' Which I think is something that she doesn't like. Then she said he asked a question about Frank's sexuality: 'Do you know what Frank's first sexual experience was?'"

In other words, he called O'Hara a lesser poet, said he was a scenester, and focused on his sex life. *He hit the faux-pas trifecta*, I thought. Just like in a fairy tale or in a sport: three chances, three wishes—three strikes, you're out.

"*I* wouldn't pull the rug out from somebody for that, but I understand why that would rub her the wrong way," said Josh. "It was that and the way that the publishers were treating her. That part doesn't seem to have a whole lot to do with him."

I said my father was kind of famous for putting his foot in his mouth, so it didn't surprise me too much.

"It's like a *Curb Your Enthusiasm* sort of scenario," Josh said, and laughed.

I told Josh that he was not the first to make a comparison between my father and Larry David. I wondered if I shouldn't give Maureen some space to mull and see how she felt and then keep her up to date on the project. He said that sounded smart to him and that she seemed to like having been consulted and asked for an interview. As I hung up the phone, I felt vindicated: it was my father's fault after all. And it looked like I would win.

I returned to listening to the tapes with renewed enthusiasm and was rewarded right away with the best Brooklyn accent I'd ever heard. Painter Jane Freilicher, née Niederhoffer, one of the New York School of painters, painted my friend and one-time babysitter Katie Schneeman topless; the picture hangs in Katie's living room at 29 St. Marks. Freilicher met Frank O'Hara in 1950 or '51 and they "all went out to *dinnah*."

Jane Freilicher—2/19/77

Jane Freilicher: My first impression was I was *stah-tled* by his whole
  style, which was very exotic to me.

Peter Schjeldahl: Was his style intact from the beginning?

JF: Well, I think, as he was younger, it seemed in a way— Could I
  show you a photograph of him? I think you might like to see it.

PS: I'd love to see it. Looks like you've got a lot of goodies there.

JF: This is the photograph I mean.

PS: Good heavens.

JF: That will give you an impression of what he was like—what he
  seemed to be like. I couldn't quite digest the fact of this great—

PS: Leaning on a rake and two mops.

JF: That was taken by George Montgomery.

PS: Probably in Cambridge.

JF: Yeah.

PS: There's paint on it, too. Nice touch.

Later in the interview, she talked about how nice O'Hara was to
have around.

JF: He was very good at any kind of manual work. He volunteered to
  do anything, helping.

PS: Odd jobs around the studio?

JF: Yeah, and he liked to do it. He just liked to hang around studios—
  my studio, Larry's studio. And he might write something there. His
  life was so casual that great passages of time went by—sort of play,
  playtime.

My father told Freilicher that O'Hara's "walking-around poems of
the late fifties seem to me totally unique in literature." He also said,
"Absolutely part of what makes him a great poet—he could take a

feeling right where it was." Then Freilicher offered to let my father read the letters O'Hara sent her. He declined, even though across the span of time I screamed at him, *Take the damn letters!*

There was a real rapport between my father and Freilicher. She persisted in being charming and offering lyrical memories even as my father pushed her for dates. She talked about studying painting in the mid-1940s.

PS: What was that like?

JF: You know, art student days. Sort of strange and wonderful. I don't know, it all seems very— I was thinking while this music was playing, the Dvořák concerto, which is so romantic—and I was thinking of my little flat I had on West Tenth Street, which was really abominable, and knowing Frank, and the sort of camaraderie of those days. It seemed very much like something out of Puccini. I was wondering if that's what young artists have now. It seems very remote.

PS: It's very hard for me to picture except as a Puccini. I don't know how I'm going to deal with it.

JF: I felt like I was Mimi or something.

[Knock on the door. She has a short exchange with a repairman.]

PS: Most things in life should be so simple.

JF: Of course, it wasn't simple. It was full of agony and struggle and poverty and—

PS: I meant the television repair.

JF: Oh, it's wonderful. They keep coming and fixing everything. Do you have it?

PS: No.

JF: We have to have it because—

PS: I'd love it.

JF: We have to have it because we can't get reception here.

PS: There are all those funky, funny cable programs.

JF: If you have access to them.

They talked about who O'Hara slept with and who he didn't.

PS: These are all things I probably wouldn't have to wonder about if I'd known him.

JF: Well, they were crucial, I suppose, to a biography, if to nothing else. [Laughs.] That's what people want to know, right—did he or didn't he? It's quite a job for you.

PS: Raking around—

JF: —in the muck. [Laughs.] You didn't know him at all? You met him?

PS: I met him. Two or three times. And I had the experience that every-one of my generation had—an incredible kindness and the quality of "taking seriously," which absolutely astounded me, to the point where I don't remember anything about him. All I remember is—

JF: Your reaction.

PS: My reaction.

This line stops me dead. My father met Frank O'Hara and what did he take away from it? Only his own reaction. How could you be so self-involved as to not see someone you care about when they're standing right in front of you?

And O'Hara was so remarkable. It seems that to know him was often to be both in love and afraid. One day at the beach, Jane Frei-licher recalls, O'Hara dove into rough surf again and again, even as down the beach an ambulance arrived to collect someone whose arm had been broken by the waves. He was a marvelous swimmer, she said. And yet there was also something terrifying about the way he swam.

PS: The romance of death—

JF: It was very big.

PS: —was very big. Especially in Frank's early poems, when he was youngest and most vibrant, it's absolutely ubiquitous.

JF: Well, he was very much in the Rimbaud mold—what is it? The *poète maudit*. And he was—I hate to sound like that horrible [literary critic] Richard Howard, but he did have a certain carelessness with his life. He did things that were very foolhardy and risky. He lived at the edge of his stamina all the time.

In his little book *I Remember*, second-generation New York School poet Joe Brainard wrote: "I remember one very cold black winter night on the beach alone with Frank O'Hara. He ran into the ocean naked and it scared me to death."

One evening when my mother was out of town and Neal was working late at his box office job, my father came to Williamsburg, and we went out for dinner with Oliver. Afterward, he came over for ice cream in the living room. Oliver went into his room to do homework.

"So," I said. "I heard from Josh that Maureen remembers me. She said you brought me once when you went to see her. Does that sound right?"

"It could be."

"Do you remember anything else about that trip?"

"It was a little tense."

"Josh said Maureen remembers some things you said that made her concerned. Do you want to know what they were?"

He closed his eyes. This is a common experience for him—hearing what he's done wrong, letting it wash over him. "What were they?"

"He said you told her that John Ashbery was a better poet. You said Frank was just the more social person, the glue that held the scene together. Then you asked if she knew about his first sexual experience. He said those were three of her biggest pet peeves: that people thought Ashbery was more talented, that O'Hara was just a partier, and anything at all to do with his sex life."

"I can see myself doing that," he said.

Chapter 9

When Vincent Warren left for Canada to work in a ballet company, O'Hara cursed the entire Canadian nation for stealing his boyfriend. In his grief, he took comfort in the company of Bill Berkson, a nineteen-year-old poet.

Berkson fit a pattern: he was good-looking, more than a decade younger, and straight, and O'Hara seemed to be in love with him. There was something about Berkson, though, that inspired more jealousy than usual in O'Hara's friends. One wrote: "One summer, in the late fifties, Frank appeared on the beach at Water Mill in the company of a very young, outrageously handsome, and sullen young man."

Berkson introduced O'Hara to Biotherm, a $12 suntan lotion, which became the subject of the late, long poem "Biotherm (for Bill Berkson)." From 1960 to 1962, O'Hara dedicated poems to Berkson, and Berkson dedicated poems to O'Hara. Together they wrote a chapbook called *Hymns of St. Bridget*, about the church off Tompkins Square Park.

O'Hara loved hearing Berkson's childhood stories of growing up rich on Fifth Avenue, the son of Eleanor Lambert, who created the

International Best Dressed List and New York Fashion Week, but my father and Berkson don't seem to get along so well.

Bill Berkson—Bolinas, California—3/31/77

Peter Schjeldahl: Who would take care of you?

Bill Berkson: Oh, I had nannies and governesses. I had one governess who lived with us for a long time, maybe ten years. And she had a lovely daughter, too, who lived with us and was like my sister and in a way probably my first love, too.

PS: Sounds like it's an at once very rich and impoverished childhood.

BB: Oh, I guess. I don't know. You mean like a poor little rich boy or something?

PS: Not quite that, no.

BB: Um.

PS: I don't want to get psychological.

BB: Yeah. I don't know.

As a freshman at Brown in 1957, Berkson became aware of *On the Road* and Henry Miller, Allen Ginsberg, and Gregory Corso, as well as the painters Jackson Pollock, Arshile Gorky, and Piet Mondrian. For Thanksgiving break, he went out to San Francisco to find the Beats. He went stumbling around North Beach saying, "Where's Allen Ginsberg?" "Where's Philip Whalen?" But the only San Francisco poet he encountered was Jack Spicer. The party was over.

Still in search of his tribe, Berkson spent that summer in Europe, though his only Beat sighting there was Gregory Corso acting up in a bar. Back at school his sophomore year, he took a short story class with John Hawkes. Hawkes mentioned some poems by Frank O'Hara in the *Evergreen Review* as poems he liked, in contrast with almost all other new poetry. Berkson discovered he liked them, too, very much.

The night before the end of Christmas vacation, he got a phone call that his father, who was a publisher at Hearst, had died. Berkson was living with some friends in an apartment off campus. He walked down the stairs with his bag. Upon seeing his housemate, he said, "My father died and I'm going to New York . . . And I don't think I'm coming back to Brown."

He moved into his mother's New York City apartment and attended the New School. He had a choice between studying poetry with Kenneth Koch or music composition with John Cage, which Berkson heard involved making songs out of coughing and dropping pencils on desks. He opted for the former. Koch made him believe it was possible to be a poet, and introduced him to O'Hara. That was in May or June 1959; they were inseparable from then until O'Hara died seven years later.

In his 2016 *New York Times* obituary, Bill Berkson is called "the ever-present third man from the left in the group photographs that chronicle the era." As he wrote in his memoir *Since When*, he was probably the only person at both the Woodstock Music Festival and Truman Capote's Black and White Masked Ball at the Plaza Hotel.

In 2019, his widow, the curator Connie Lewallen, agreed to meet with me and to show me Berkson's brand-new posthumous book, a beautifully reproduced notebook he'd kept with stories about and souvenirs of Frank O'Hara. We did not know it then but days later the book would get a rave review in the *Washington Post*.

Lewallen said, "Even though Frank was so important to Bill—inspired him, encouraged him—that Bill came along in Frank's life when he did was really helpful to Frank. Kind of inspired him. Because Frank had been so busy as a curator and wasn't really doing a lot of writing. It wasn't just a completely one-way street."

She asked me to tell her more about my project.

When I finished explaining to Lewallen about the tapes she said, "You must know Spencer?" She'd heard that he and my father were friends.

I said yes.

She said, "Spencer was in Bill's class. A number of years ago, Bill said, 'You know, I have this student. He's very young. He's read every-thing. He comes from this very unexpected background considering what he's read and what he knows.' He didn't often talk about his students much, but this one he talked about. So, then we got to know Spencer. It was funny because he came here to go to graduate school, and he quit. Me, being a mother, I said, 'No! You can't quit. You've got to get your degree.' I remember saying that as if he were my son. Of course, it turns out he was completely fine without that degree because he's kind of extra special."

There's no beating Spencer, I thought. *He's the good son even when he's dropping out of school.*

Berkson left New York just four years after O'Hara's death, and he stayed in California from 1970 on except for the many trips he and Lewallen took around the world, including two weeks in Istanbul after a successful lung transplant. And he kept doing readings, often from his long poem "Costanza":

> A woman has fallen the museum guard
> Tells us in a light blue turban plus dark suit . . .

"Bill finally retired," Lewallen said. "He continued to teach sem-inars. He did more writing in the last twelve years of his life, he said, than he had in the previous twenty. That's because he had this renewed energy. And also because, although he never said it, I think he knew that he was a little bit on borrowed time. He just wanted to keep writing, keep writing, keep writing."

In 2009, Berkson published his book of collected poems, *Portrait and Dream*. Although he joked: "Who's going to read these? Someone said that at any given time, there are only about twenty poets that are read."

The artist George Schneeman painted nude portraits of a number of poets, including my father and Bill Berkson. Lewallen tells me that Berkson wanted to hang the gigantic full-frontal portrait of himself in their home, but there wasn't a wall big enough. Now it's in the collection of the Berkeley Art Museum and Pacific Film Archive.

Berkson was proud of that painting and yet he was a little tired of being called handsome all the time. "Bill didn't want to be known as handsome," Lewallen told me. "He wanted to be known as a really great writer."

But what can you do? He was absurdly handsome.

Being known for that, Lewallen grants, smiling: "It's not the worst thing in the world."

A student in Bill Berkson's 1966 New School class, Frances LeFevre, sent letters to her daughter, the poet Anne Waldman. Those letters have been collected into a small press book called *Dearest Annie*. In one of the first letters, LeFevre observes my father arguing passionately with Berkson after class: "Noticed P. Scheldahjl [*sic*] having serious discussion with B. after getting his own papers back and heard him say, 'Yes, but I'm very serious about what I'm trying to do . . .' B. kept apparently saying something to him and he didn't look very happy—but then he has a sad face anyhow."

I knew my father had studied with Koch, but I didn't know he studied with Berkson, too. LeFevre later said that my father's love of John Ashbery's poetry was "unthinking worship . . . Scheldahjl [*sic*] doesn't seem to have much humor and looks so *sad* and ashen all the time. I'd like to put him under a sun lamp for a couple of hours." She also suspected he was in love with their fellow classmate Bernadette Mayer, which he was.

Mayer would become close friends with Waldman, who would move to 33 St. Marks Place. She ran the St. Mark's Poetry Project from 1966 to 1978 and published my father's poetry collection *Dreams* as part of her Angel Hair Books press.

Waldman's neighbors at 29 St. Marks Place were my parents' close friends George and Katie Schneeman. Katie took care of me sometimes when I was a baby. I still stop in to see her every few months. On one of these visits, Katie told me that after my father's first wife, Linda, died in 2011, she was cleaning out Linda's place and discovered a file on me with articles I'd written and my wedding announcement.

Katie said that Linda thought of me as the child she never had. On Linda's second date with my father, she'd become pregnant; a backstreet abortion in Chicago had left her unable to ever bear children. Linda was a poet, and her work had appeared in some of the same anthologies as my father's had in the 1960s. But after their divorce she stopped writing poetry and became a copy editor. When she died, there was no obituary in the *New York Times* or in any paper that I could find. I felt sad for her and strange. All these years I was being watched without knowing it.

Chapter 10

One night in the 1970s at St. Mark's Poetry Project, my father did a reading of what he thought were his best-ever poems. No one laughed, even at the funniest lines. When he finished reading, the applause was feeble. The audience seemed dejected, maybe even angry.

"That was really . . . good," someone chastised him on his way out.

By that time O'Hara had gone somewhat out of fashion. In the *New York Herald Tribune*, John Ashbery wrote that O'Hara might be "too hip for the squares and too square for the hips."

In 1985, my father wrote a letter to the *New York Times* explaining exactly how he felt about the post-O'Hara poetry scene.

The rise of serious pop songwriting two decades ago usurped poetry's last, most vulgar and least dispensable function in society, the articulation of youthful feeling . . . Until poetry of some kind again grips the imaginations of the young—as painting, its sister art, lately has to a surprising extent—poetry will remain a quaint pursuit limited to bland coteries and the death embrace of academe. Until then, discussions of form and quality will have a hollow ring. When a job has no social consequence, who cares if it is done well or badly? How today would we qualify a "good" buggy whip?

By contrast, Kenneth Koch, O'Hara's contemporary and my father's teacher, wrote and taught poetry for the rest of his life.

In 2019, Koch's widow, Karen, opened the door to her apartment near Columbia University. Wearing dark pants and a brown sweater, her bob swaying lightly, she looked too pretty and too calm to be attached to the downtown poetry world, and yet her apartment resembled a New York School museum. She showed me around, brought out snacks, and gave me copies of Koch's books. We talked for a couple of hours. She explained how she recruited a team to help her manage Koch's estate. She showed off the collections and laughed when she pulled out one that had turned out a little differently than she'd expected. The blue and orange were so bright that the book looked like Mets swag. She was okay with it. She seemed okay with everything. I adored her.

Ron Padgett would later tell me: "She's not only a great person but also a very good literary executor, especially as a person who was not highly connected to the publishing industry. She's gone really way out there to make Kenneth's work available. She's been great at it. She's generous and helpful. She tries to find a way to say yes to every request."

The executorship team she put together was diverse in terms of age and skillset. "The good thing is that when I die and Karen dies, these guys will be younger, and they're already signed on for the long haul," Padgett said. "So, she's provided as far down the road as she can. Everybody should have such a literary executor as Karen."

I made a mental note that my mother and I should emulate Karen when it came to my father's estate. I could assemble a team with people who knew different aspects of his work and who were a range of ages, like Ron and Spencer. Together we'd be able to keep his work and legacy alive for the foreseeable future.

Karen met Kenneth in 1977, the same year my father was trying to write his book. She was running an education consulting agency and loved his books about teaching poetry. Her company had a grant to spend, so she hired him to work with teachers on their writing curriculums. They started dating in the eighties and spent weekends in Southampton playing music with Larry Rivers.

She felt she got Koch's best years: "He was past a lot of his difficult times at that point. I'll say that's also true of your father, probably."

I agreed.

"I don't think he liked Kenneth very much," she said without malice.

"I don't know about that, but I do know he's a huge fan of his writing," I said. "I was talking to him the other day, and he said that one of his favorite poems of all time was—"

Karen interrupted me: "I've got to guess. I'm going to guess! 'Variations on a Theme' by William Carlos Williams?"

"No, that's one of *my* favorites," I said.

"Oh! I just wanted to make the guess. Go ahead, please."

"It's actually really funny because I was at dinner at my parents', and I quoted that poem. My father said, 'Oh, that's a good one, but an even better one is the one where he's doing a Robert Frost impression."

"Ah! 'Mending Sump'!"

"Yes, exactly. And his favorite line is: 'Hay is dried-up grass when you're alone.'"

She laughed a charming laugh. "I'd forgotten that line. Thank you for reminding me."

"My dad quotes it all the time. I do think he cared for him, but I wouldn't be surprised if there was some sort of difficulty."

"Kenneth says when he was younger, he sometimes made some enemies."

"Well, so did my father."

"I think that happens to people with strong personalities."

When I said something about the Village being full of strong personalities, she said, "I'm such a Midwestern girl, I think. I'm an amateur musician, a pianist. Kenneth used to have his office in here. When he died, I decided I had to make the living room my own. The apartment already is sort of a shrine to him." She put her piano in the space formerly occupied by his desk.

Karen Koch even gets along with Maureen. "She's really wonderful," Koch said, though she admitted that Maureen could be protective.

She told me that Kenneth Koch, along with Larry Rivers and Bill Berkson, went to O'Hara's apartment after he died and made photocopies of every scrap of paper because they were afraid otherwise some of the more explicit work would be lost: "They pulled everything because they were afraid at that time, Maureen would not have liked—and she said as much, actually—his being gay was not something that she wanted to really put out there. She just needed time to adjust to the grandeur of Frank, I think."

She talked about the poets' "groupness." "Jane [Freilicher] was hard as nails and wonderful," Koch says. "She didn't pull her punches ever. She was great with me. After Kenneth died, being out in Long Island, I spent quite a bit of time with her. When Kenneth was in the hospital, she would call me at night just to catch up. One night I said, 'Well, they have to shave his head.' She said, 'Oh, but he has a really nicely shaped head! He'll look fine.'"

When Freilicher was dying, Koch went to sit with her for a couple of hours: "I got some books and I started reading John's and Frank's—I couldn't find a James Schuyler—and Kenneth's poems to her. I kept reading them to her and she was kind of responding even though . . . I still remember she was sort of propped up in bed. Her hair was flowing across the pillow like in a Pre-Raphaelite painting. She had this regal bearing. I finished reading. She looked tired. I said, 'You know, Jane? Those guys really loved you. They really, really loved you.' No one was there with me. She pushed back on the pillow and said, more or less, it sounded like, 'I love them!'"

Freilicher died the next day.

I leave half in love with Karen and convinced that if she thought I stood a chance of getting Maureen to support my project, it must be true.

And yet, Maureen still hadn't written me back. I sent her my "journalist inquiry" on January 10. I followed up with my book proposal on February 1 and asked if I could take her out for lunch or coffee that month. A week after that, I wrote her to say that Katie Schneeman, whom she'd met many years earlier, sent her regards. Weeks passed, and nothing.

Chapter 11

While I wait to hear from Maureen, I listen to an interview my father did with her and Frank's brother, Philip.

Right away, I notice how hard Philip and his wife, Ariel, are trying to please. They pull out poetry books and yearbooks and discuss family dynamics, histories, motivations. They tell my father they'll help him track down one of O'Hara's favorite childhood playmates, and put him in touch with a cousin who has the family's whole gene-alogy. And they roll with my father's lack of confidence. I don't know that I'd be as patient.

Philip and Ariel O'Hara—Oak Park, Illinois—4/14/77
Peter Schjeldahl: Let's see. Do you want to— Should we experiment
  with on the record / off the record?
Philip O'Hara: If I say off the record, you can stop the machine, okay?
PS: Okay. All right . . . Otherwise it's on the record?
PO: Yep. Took a long time to establish that, but at least we got it
  worked out. Go ahead, Peter.

★   ★   ★

One reporter friend of mine writes sensitive national security stories. I asked her once about best practices for going off the record. She said that as a reporter you are in control of the interview, and you set the ground rules. She identifies herself to her subject as a reporter. The interview subject tells her things with that understanding. If he starts to tell her something is off the record, she says, "No, wait! If you don't want this in print, please don't tell it to me. I'm a reporter, and I only want to know things I can write down. Please just tell me things that I can use." She says often the person will then say all the same things he would have anyway, but she will have it properly sourced and doesn't have to sort out later what's fair game and what's not.

My father doesn't seem to have the experience to take control like that. It seems his confidence has been rattled by how much harder this project is than he thought it would be. I hear a weariness in his voice every time Maureen's name comes up.

He's giving her too much power, I think, and he's creating a fight where there doesn't need to be one. If he'd just be nicer to her, I'm sure she'd come around. In any case, he should stop being so distracted. He should notice all the good that is there instead.

Philip is full of details about O'Hara that I've never heard before. Their parents met when their father, Russell, was the college English teacher of their mother, Kay. One of Kay's brothers was killed driving a Coca-Cola truck when he lost control and crashed near the family home. One of her sisters was a librarian who died of brain cancer. Another sister, a nun and English teacher, died of tuberculosis. (Philip says the archdiocese didn't give her proper medical care and he's still angry about it.) Frank and Philip's maternal grandmother's brother, J. Frank Donahue, owned much of the real estate in Grafton. The Donahue company also had a hand in livestock, farm equipment, and undertaking. One of the family's favorite stories was of the time when, in the field behind their home at 6 North Street, an eagle swooped down and carried off a black lamb.

I love all these details, and I love how expansive Philip is in discussing the family. He repeatedly talks about how women in the family were "typical ghetto Irish Catholic victims." There was a long tradition in the family of intellectual maiden aunts. He says Russell's sister Grace was among the women who denied her own dreams in order to serve as caregiver for her parents. She and other aunts gave Frank, firstborn of the firstborn, countless books with loving dedications in the front. They made his education their business.

Polar opposites in almost every way, Frank and Philip never saw eye to eye about the family. Over drinks at the Gotham Bar in Manhattan as late as 1965, Frank told him that he hated their mother. Philip insisted that while she'd had problems, she was a stronger advocate for Frank than his father had been and a force for good in his life. She insisted he play the piano, be refined, have a social life. In high school, he was even able to audit classes at the New England Conservatory in Boston, where he likely would have pursued a degree if he hadn't been called to war. What's more, Philip argued that their mother was an interesting person. As a Girl Scout troop leader, she'd caught hell once for trying to teach the girls about different religions, going so far as to take them on an unauthorized field trip to a synagogue.

Frank was unmoved, Philip said. He hated Grafton, though Philip didn't quite understand why. Frank said, "Well, Phil, when you're older you'll understand." And Philip said, "I'm sure I will, but I don't now."

PS: So your earliest memory of Frank was that he was going off to parochial school and what else?

PO: Well, you know, Frank and I lived two totally different lives. It was like we lived in different families. I'm really reaching in my recollection, but he was the most beautifully dressed kid that went off to school every day. My mother had always taught him to be polite and be nice. And I'll never forget the day that a kid took a piece of birch wood and broke his nose. And my mother had told Frank never to fight back. And so Frank didn't get his nose broken once; he got it broken twice.

PS: By the same kid?

PO: Yes. And Frank never lifted a finger to defend himself.

Broken twice! By the same kid! O'Hara's nose would be crooked for the rest of his life—a testimony to his mother's pacifism.

Philip said he always regretted that the family sold a piece of farmland they owned in Grafton called Tower Hill. Before he went to the navy, Frank had asked the family to save it for him because he wanted to raise English and Irish setters there. When they sold it, Philip says, it broke Frank's heart. And yet, for the sake of American letters, it's probably better that after the war Frank went to Harvard and then New York City instead of becoming a dog breeder on Tower Hill.

When Frank's father, Russell, died at age forty-eight of a heart attack at a bowling alley, Frank came home from Harvard for the funeral. "Frank was totally emotionless, like a goddamn zombie," Philip says of Frank's demeanor after their father's death. "We waked my father in our house, typical Irish wake. And then all of a sudden, we heard these gargantuan screams and cries. It was Frank upstairs in his own room. It took a great deal of effort to calm him down. It had built up in him for so long."

Russell hadn't left a will or prepared Kay to take care of herself, so Philip reported that his aunt Grace moved in and criticized everything Kay did. The family liquidated the Donahue company. Philip, who was fourteen at the time, believed his mother was given far less than her due, and he resented Frank, then twenty-one, for not stepping in and protecting her interests.

Around this time, Kay started drinking heavily and left the children to their own devices. I can't imagine what they went through, raising themselves after dealing with so much trauma. Philip scraped together the money for Maureen's private-school education (Frank chipped in what little he had), asking a couple of local people to cosign notes and borrowing from the schools. He tells my father with pride in his voice that he paid it all back when she graduated.

Frank sent his little brother and sister cards and letters while he was in the navy. Maureen, a refined and pretty little girl, adored her brother and took to heart his advice on what books to read and what music to listen to. But Frank didn't return home often, and when he did, he avoided talking about what he'd seen in the war. The only thing Philip remembers him saying was that Philip's canary had to be sent away because its chirping reminded Frank too much of the sonar beeps he'd lived with on the ship.

PS: He was at one point a lookout for planes because he was particularly sharp-eyed and could identify any model of plane from a long distance. He said he used to lay awake at night worrying that he was going to be responsible for the shooting down of the next great Japanese composer.

PO: Is that right? That's a story I haven't heard.

PS: He was already more interested in art than in war or politics.

PO: One of the greatest stories I remember about him was . . . I was in the army. I was on my way to Korea. It was 1953. And he invited me to New York for the weekend. And I arrived and he lived on Forty-Ninth Street. Right by the Great Gatsby's, right there by the UN Building. He'd been shot. Have you heard this story? He lived on the fourth floor—

PS: He was shot while you were there?

PO: Oh, yes.

PS: Give me your memory of that event.

PO: And so, I came in and there were all kinds of police guys there. I knew goddamn well this was his room. I walked in the room. It was a fourth-floor walkup, and I'd never been in the room before.

PS: And this is just when you arrived?

PO: Yes, absolutely.

PS: And he'd just been shot?

PO: Yes! Minutes before. Twenty minutes before, ten minutes before. I'd taken a bus to the West Side Terminal from Fort Dix, New Jersey. I walked in and all the goddamned lights in the world are on, and Frank is sitting on a wooden chair like that ladder-back chair, but not as nice. And he's naked except for a towel around his bottom. And there's a doctor and nurse around and lots of police.

The tape stopped there, but my father paid a second visit to Illinois a couple of months later and heard the rest.

He seems even more hesitant on this trip. He repeats a number of questions that were answered on the first trip. He asks how he might get in touch with one of Frank's childhood friends, forgetting that he was told on the first visit she'd committed suicide. Nevertheless, Philip and Ariel seem even chattier than before.

Philip and Ariel O'Hara—Oak Park, Illinois—6/16/77

Ariel O'Hara: Was he drafted?

PO: No, he volunteered immediately after he graduated. And that's interesting. My mother insisted that he not be in the trenches. She wouldn't stand for him being in the army. She wanted him to have a—she was a big clean-sheet person. In the navy, you may get torpedoed and go down to Davy Jones, but you'll go down with clean sheets. [Laughs.]

PS: You'll have clean underwear on.

Philip continues the earlier story of the shooting.

PO: What happened was he told me he was accosted by four boys.
He'd been to a delicatessen by the Belmont Plaza to buy food for us
for the weekend. And he was accosted by four kids. He hit one with
a bottle of milk and then he ran. He heard a shot. Felt nothing. In
the hallway he felt something warm going down his leg. He had a
raincoat, trench coat on. Of course, when he got into the apartment,
he realized it was blood. He called the building super. Anyway, I got
in a huge fight with the nurse and medical guy there. They said he'd
been stabbed. I said, "Jesus Christ, it's a bullet wound. You can see
the puncture in the skin." And I got the raincoat and showed them
the hollow mark. They still refused to believe me. He was terribly
angry with me that I was being so uppity with the authorities [who
said] that it had to be a stab.

Philip took his wounded brother to the hospital at Welfare Island.
Then he went back to the apartment and, scared to be alone in the
city at night, turned on all the lights. At four o'clock in the morning
the telephone rang. The detective asked Philip how he was. He said,
"I'm so goddamned scared. Every noise I hear I'm ready to jump out
a window." The detective said, "We're watching the building." Philip
said, "Shit, that doesn't make me feel any better."

I could listen to Philip talk about his brother forever. I'm starting
to get a sense of the characters in O'Hara's orbit. When Philip says
Frank's friends showed up the next day to take over, I'm not surprised
by the list of caretakers: Grace Hartigan, Jane Freilicher, Hal Fondren,
James Schuyler, John Ashbery.

Philip went back to Fort Dix. The bullet wasn't removed because
it was embedded in the muscle—something that would cause pain
later in life.

When, thirteen years later, O'Hara was hit by the dune buggy on Fire Island, Philip took a midnight flight to be at his brother's side in the hospital. He said Frank told him: "Phil, why did you come? Go home and take care of Ariel and the kids. I'll be out in the morning." Philip says Frank was dead twenty minutes later.

The ensuing melodrama poisoned Philip against many of Frank's friends. Philip particularly hated Patsy Southgate, whose apartment became the group's headquarters in the days that followed O'Hara's death. Everyone was drunk and unhinged, he said, with Southgate's young children there, taking it all in. In response to some complaint of his, Southgate told him it would have been better if Philip, not Frank, had been crushed under the dune buggy's tires. Philip says he had to fight for permission to invite his and Frank's mother to the funeral.

PS: Whose idea was it that Kay not be invited?

PO: All of them. The idea was he hated her, and she wouldn't be there, including Maureen.

PS: Including Maureen?

PO: Yes. Oh, yes. And I just told them that she was going to be there or there'd be no funeral.

AO: You have to interject to say that had been a particularly bad time for Kay. That whole period.

PO: She was institutionalized.

AO: And it was a particularly devastating time for Kay, which had all kinds of ramifications for people that that affected.

PO: My view was the mother of the child— I don't give a shit if she was a felon—

PS: Yeah, when you die, your mother gets to come.

PO: That was my position.

I'm struck by what Philip says here, something I know I must have heard before but that hasn't sunk in until now: Frank O'Hara didn't choose Maureen as his executor. He died with no will. That meant it was up to Kay, Philip, and Maureen, as next of kin, to figure out what to do with the estate. Kay was not considered competent, so only one question remained: would the estate go to Philip or Maureen?

Philip told my father that when it came to the executor job, "I said whatever Maureen wanted was fine with me." The main thing he said he wanted was for his brother to have a proper funeral, with a real burial in a real cemetery and the whole immediate family there, including their mother.

He got his way. Kay arrived at the funeral looking every inch the elegant New England matriarch. With her hazel eyes and impeccable outfit, she stood out against the crowd of poets and painters who wept like children and drank like sailors.

Maureen, then twenty-nine, became their brother's literary executor, with the power to act on O'Hara's behalf when negotiating contracts with publishers, renewing copyrights, and collecting royalties. From then on, she would be the sole decision maker when anybody sought to quote from his work beyond the limited lines allowed according to the doctrine of fair use. For the rest of her life, unless she handed over control, she would act as the sole guardian of her late brother's reputation and legacy.

Even though she was younger than almost everyone else at the funeral, Maureen probably did seem the most grown-up. Philip shared the opinion later expressed by O'Hara's friend Ned Rorem in *Gay Sunshine* magazine: "Frank O'Hara died, and New York City was overrun with widows of all sexes. I've never seen such spiteful behavior. The number of people who acted like barnyard creatures gnashing at each other instead of coming together in a common cause. Each one said, 'Frank loved me the most. Frank gave me this poem.'"

Philip returned to Illinois furious at his brother's friends, and at what he called the joke of a hospital out on Fire Island that let his brother die without proper treatment, and at what he considered insufficient consequences for the kid driving the dune buggy. He even wrote to Governor Nelson Rockefeller demanding a ban on Fire Island dune buggies—an effort that he says was "magnificently unsuccessful."

After he'd fought all the battles he could think to fight, Philip finally mourned his brother. One was a lean cosmopolitan poet, the other a heavy suburban businessman. They didn't agree about their mother, nor about Grafton. But for the last five or six years of Frank's life, the two had started going out together once a month or so, to the Gotham Bar, the Five Spot, the Jazz Gallery. They went to Italian restaurants. They played bocce. And Philip liked some of his brother's friends very much, especially the beautiful painters Jane Freilicher and Grace Hartigan.

A decade after Frank's death, in Philip and Ariel's house in Oak Park, wind chimes sound in the distance, teenage children run in and out of the room, and a new pet canary chirps. Philip tells my father: "We didn't have a lot in common, but we got along pretty well."

On our best days, that's what I think about my father. And I think that while we don't have very many things in common, we do have the best things: writing and books and Frank O'Hara.

On one of my father's two trips to Oak Park, Philip and Ariel let him go down into their basement to look at the five hundred books they'd saved of O'Hara's collection.

My father talks into his tape recorder while looking through them. There are papers tucked into some of them: a list of kennels specializing in Afghan hounds; fragments of poems; photographs, including one of the British poet Steven Spender; a postcard from Edward Gorey. Many are gifts from his parents—"For our dearest son"—or from his aunt Mary or aunt Grace or other relatives. On the title pages, O'Hara notes where he read the books and what the year was.

Philip and Ariel O'Hara—O'Hara's pre-1950s Library—1977
PS: *Sinister Street* by Compton McKenzie. Harvard '47. *Out of Africa* by Isak Dinesen. Grafton '47. *Winter Words in Various Moods and Meters* by Thomas Hardy. Harvard '48. Here's something interesting: *The Theory and Practice of Strict Counterpoint* by Victor von Lytle, Musical Doctor. Ditson Company. Philadelphia. 1940. I think. Yeah. Inscribed Francis O'Hara. Los Angeles 1946. Tucked into the book, a neatly typed transcription of a passage from *The Dead* by James Joyce. It starts, "A few light taps upon the pane made him turn toward the window," and ends, "faintly falling like the descent of their last end upon all the living and the dead."

Chapter 12

The more they're about writing, the better I like these tapes. Like Frank O'Hara, I was the sort of child to whom people gave books. One day a family friend gave me Edward Gorey's *Amphigorey Also*, no doubt because as a skinny child who liked looking out windows, I was a natural reader for Gorey's Victorian rhymes and morbid pen-and-ink illustrations. In his books, which I did enjoy, children are always being eaten by mice or drowned in lakes or carried off by illness.

Gorey grew up in Chicago, where he was in the same high school class as the painter Joan Mitchell, who would later live near us on St. Marks Place. His spooky style was in place even before, in old age, his long white beard completed the picture—earrings, lots of rings, fur coat, sneakers. O'Hara said Gorey was the first person ever to wear sneakers with dress-up clothes. He didn't fit in with the Harvard veterans for a number of reasons; among them, he wore his hair in little bangs and was "yawningly uninterested in sex," according to his biographer. At Harvard there were rumors about him being, among other suspicious things, a virgin.

O'Hara and Gorey bonded over their love of the ballet and of the witty British novelist Ronald Firbank, and they staged avant-garde plays together in Cambridge at the Poets' Theatre, a small performance space over a hardware store.

When they both moved to New York in the early fifties, Gorey worked as an illustrator and author, self-publishing his first books and selling them directly through Midtown's Gotham Book Mart bookstore, which is where my father interviews him as classical music plays in the background. Gorey starts off sounding nervous.

Edward Gorey—Gotham Book Mart, Midtown, New York City
(41 West Forty-Seventh Street) —6/26/77

Edward Gorey: As I remember, you know, Frank was, you know, I mean, I, well, I don't know how serious either one of us were about, you know, writing as a career or anything at that time. We were just sort of, I just remember, sort of, you know, having fun, as it were. And Frank, you know, Frank was terrifically prol— You know, he really ground out those, some of those poems *very rapidly indeed*. And there's not much revision and so forth and so on.

Gorey says his and O'Hara's methods of writing were entirely different. He struggled, while O'Hara would "sit down and *tweedle, tweedle, tweedle*, write another three-page poem, then off to the movies." I've never before heard the sound of a typewriter represented as *"tweedle, tweedle, tweedle,"* but Gorey always was fanciful.

Gorey seems to look down on O'Hara—and on nearly everyone else, too—except husky-voiced Bunny Lang, whom he adored, insisting that she, more than O'Hara, seemed like the member of their Harvard clique who would and should become famous.

When O'Hara, Gorey, and Lang put on their plays together, Lang was famous for, in one instance, having learned not one line of her dialogue. She sat there onstage in a hostess gown, playing with pearls, having each line fed to her until, Gorey says with a laugh, the entire audience wanted her dead.

She had an affair with the abstract expressionist painter Mike Goldberg, who asked her patrician father for her hand in marriage. Mr. Lang was having none of it, in part because Bunny had Hodgkin's disease and needed more looking after than Goldberg could manage.

In an essay, O'Hara recalled the first time he saw Bunny: across the room at a Cambridge cocktail party in a bookstore. She was sulking in a corner, wearing a Roman-striped skirt. The girl he was talking to said, "That's Bunny Lang. I'd like to give her a good slap." He wrote about her often. In "A Mexican Guitar," he calls her "a mysteriosabelle."

When the Harvard crowd went swimming at Marblehead Rock, someone tried to tell her it wasn't safe to dive. Before plunging into the water, she recited these lines from the British poet Ben Jonson:

> And this Security,
> It is the common moth
> That eats on wits and arts, and quite destroys them both.

That was how she earned the nickname Miss Marblehead Rock of 1954.

Their Harvard clique was obsessed with "art with a capital A," Gorey said. They spent a lot of time at concerts and in bookstores, conducting all-night bridge games, and drinking Lloyd's gin, the cheapest booze they could find. Gorey believed that the relationship would continue once they reconvened in New York City postgraduation, but by then O'Hara had new friends.

EG: The thing about Frank, which I'm sure you've heard before from other people— You would say, "I'm coming down to New York." And he would say, "Oh, meet me—the minute you get here, come down

to the [San] Remo." People who didn't really know New York terribly all that well or have a great many friends—which was the case of
me—would come down. Then Frank would say, "Oh, hi," and possibly
throw his arms around you or possibly not. And he was perfectly capable of ignoring you for the rest of the evening, as if you had just come
in from down the street, which sometimes annoyed people consider-
ably. The one thing about Frank was that he was so totally in the present all the time, I guess. I think I said this a long time ago, and I may
just be fantasizing: I was always surprised that Frank lived as long as
he did. Not that I felt that he was particularly accident-prone, exactly,
or catastrophe-prone in that sense. I didn't really feel that. It was just
that he never seemed to realize or never seemed to want to admit that
anything he did had any consequences beyond the immediate.

In other words: Safety third.

Like many members of that Harvard contingent, Gorey became
disillusioned with O'Hara. Larry Osgood says the split came because
Gorey was offended when, upon seeing Gorey's first published book,
O'Hara said to his old friend: "Still drawing that funny little man, are
you?"

Peter Schjeldahl: Somebody told me that you once told Frank a rather
   grim vision or dream you'd had about him that upset him very
   much, that he was going to die violently.
EG: Really? I don't remember it. [Laughs.]
PS: It seemed to have hit the bull's-eye of his superstition or
   something.
EG: Really? How funny. I don't remember this at all. I mean, I can only
   imagine that I might have had some loopy dream and said, "Listen,
   kid, I had this dream that you were disemboweled by wild horses."
   I can't imagine. I'm not given to having visions about people or

anything. You know, more and more I think, you know, what one person will remember about someone and what someone else will remember is very— [Opera gets very loud in background.]
PS: I think that might interfere with my recording.
EG: [To bookstore employee] Down, Gordon, down!

Gorey died in the year 2000 at the age of seventy-five. He spent his final years living with several cats on Cape Cod, in a cluttered house with poison ivy poking through the walls. Bunny Lang died in 1956 at the age of thirty-two. The Gotham Book Mart closed in 2006. The Poets' Theatre was destroyed in a fire in 1962 but was resurrected in the mid-1980s—its reopening heralded by a poster created by Edward Gorey showing some of his "funny little men" rising from their graves.

Around that time, the nearby Strand bookstore was doing a brisk business in Edward Gorey books (*The Wuggly Ump, The Gashlycrumb Tinies, The Curious Sofa*), and I was on St. Marks Place dressing up for Halloween as charismatic, mustachioed New York Mets first baseman Keith Hernandez.

When I was in elementary school, my parents took delight in making my Halloween costumes each year with a ten-dollar budget using papier-mâché and old sheets decorated with acrylic paint. My Statue of Liberty torch contained a flashlight; the cardboard tablet was hollow, for candy. My skeleton costume was a suit of white long underwear with painted-on black bones. All were paired with my usual Velcro sneakers. But the Keith Hernandez costume was special because that team was special.

Usually, the Yankees were winners and the Mets were underdogs whom we loved in spite of and maybe sometimes because of their messiness. Only this incarnation of the Mets, still awkward and scrappy but somehow also unstoppable, won the World Series. *Those* funny little men rose from their graves, too.

Chapter 13

One Saturday when my parents were upstate, I went to their empty apartment on St. Marks Place to work for a couple of hours and eat some takeout borscht from Veselka, the Ukrainian restaurant around the corner.

I walked in the front door and looked around at the elaborate mural that covered the entire hallway. A few years earlier, my mother had first painted the whole hall mustard yellow and then decorated it, including the ceiling, with hundreds of hand-painted flowers of various colors, in the style of New York School artist Joe Brainard. When I'd arrived during its creation, I asked my mother how she had the energy and attention required for that amount of grueling, detailed work. She said she'd been taking some amazing vitamins. I asked to see them. I inspected the bottle and learned that the "vitamin" was actually the dangerous diet drug fen-phen. Ever the killjoy, I told her she had to stop taking it.

After going through the addled hallway to the living room, I propped a front window open with a slide rule, filling the musty space with fresh air. The street below was blocked to traffic because a dance parade was to come through later and end in Tompkins Square Park.

Police officers in full navy-blue uniforms walked up and down the middle of the empty street. It felt strange that there was no crosstown bus rattling the windows. The garish new condo building across the street was full of non-bohemian occupants parading before their mirrors, fully visible through their giant windows.

This is the same room where I'd posed for pictures as Keith Hernandez and where my father had done the interview with O'Hara's friend Donald Droll, during which I and our incredibly annoying cat, Meow, made an unwelcome appearance.

> Donald Droll—East Village, New York City (53 St. Marks Place)—10/19/77
>
> Peter Schjeldahl: This puts Frank in the eyes of downtown in a considerable position of power. How did he handle that?
>
> Donald Droll: Well, I think Frank handled it the way—
>
> Ada Calhoun: Dah-dee!
>
> DD: I don't think he ever used it as power. I think—
>
> PS: No, but—
>
> Meow: Meow!
>
> PS: —in terms of perception of him.
>
> DD: I think a lot of people who— *Hi there!*
>
> PS: Oh. [He shuts off the recorder.]

Now, forty years later, here I am listening to these tapes. As the parade blares below, I push Play on an interview conducted with Donald Allen in the remote California art-colony town of Bolinas.

Allen assembled the anthology that first made my father aware of Frank O'Hara. And as I listen to Allen talk, I'm struck by what a good job my father did tracking all these people down and making them sit in front of his recorder. I also marvel that he did so much traveling for this book—to California, Long Island, Illinois—with a one-year-old at home, no less. He invested so much in this project—even spent a lot of money, he tells Donald Allen, on his tape recorder.

Donald Allen—Bolinas, California—3/31/77

Donald Allen: What make is it?

Peter Schjeldahl: Sony. When I started to do the book, in the midst of my complete insecurity, I determined to go out and buy the best tape recorder I could, to make myself feel better.

DA: And it operates from a battery?

PS: Yeah.

He lets Allen drift into a long history of publishing in the early 1950s. The relevant upshot is that Allen worked at Barney Rosset's Grove Press. At this, my ears perk up, because Grove was publishing my January 2020 book about Generation X.

After the Grove history, there's more about the poetry scene, and I'm mostly tuning out until I hear this:

DA: My relationship with Frank was always, although we were good friends and I saw a great deal of him socially—

PS: I know from his appointment books that I see you pop up sometimes twice a day.

DA: But our relationship was essentially editor and writer, and I commissioned some things like that review of *Dr. Zhivago* for *Evergreen*. We did spend several weekends, perhaps more than several, on Long Island—I mean at East Hampton, or at other parts of Long Island.

PS: Who did you stay with?

DA: Well, we stayed one weekend, the first weekend, with Mike [Goldberg] and Norman [Bluhm]. It's at the house that Bill de Kooning has now. And I remember we went and poured a libation of bourbon on

[Jackson] Pollock's grave. I did that more recently with Patsy [Southgate] over Frank's grave.

Hold on. Did my father say he had *O'Hara's appointment books*?

I email my father to ask. He tells me they might be in his office and that he'll check. If not, he thinks perhaps he gave them to Amei Wallach.

The next time I'm over for dinner he says he can't find the appointment books, but he carries a dozen metal notecard boxes out of his office, then stacks them on the kitchen counter. He says he's not sure what they are but he thinks they belonged to Frank O'Hara.

I take them home in a taxi in a Duane Reade bag, so afraid I'll lose them that I hold them to my chest the whole ride.

When I line them up on my coffee table and begin looking through them, I discover that they're Donald Allen's typewritten index cards, one for each of O'Hara's poems. This must have been how he assembled the *Collected Poems*. I vow to reach out to Allen's archive at the UC San Diego Library to repatriate the boxes. Meanwhile, I'm determined to find those appointment books, so I email Amei Wallach. She says I can stop by, and she will give me whatever she can find.

When I arrive at Wallach's Upper West Side apartment, she hands me a stiff drink and a folder of papers. No dice on the appointment books, but there are some great unpublished interviews. She says I can keep all the material if I promise to email her scans of her interviews and if I will deliver a folder of Fairfield Porter letters she somehow ended up with to the proper archive. Then we sit down in front of a plate of olives and nuts and chat about Frank O'Hara until it's time for me to go pick up Oliver from school.

Wallach got the idea for her Frank O'Hara book from a show put on by the Whitney Museum's curatorial program. The students did a show of Frank O'Hara and artists. "I loved the crossover between the poetry and art, so I wrote about it," Wallach says. "Then I decided it would be a really great book, and I started doing interviews."

She sold the proposal to W. W. Norton for a $20,000 advance. In the beginning, Maureen was on board but then as the months went on, "she was slowly pulling back and then I think there was a letter that said, 'No, you're not going to have permission for anything.'"

Like my father, Wallach got to keep the first part of her advance, but the book was canceled.

After getting a little drunk, I leave Wallach's apartment and head downtown. On the subway, I pull out a folder and start reading a long interview she did about O'Hara in the 1980s with Bob Dash, a poet and painter and a good friend of my mother's.

My parents spent their honeymoon at Dash's famous landmarked garden, the Madoo Conservancy in Sagaponack. I remember going there once when I was a little girl. I loved the hollyhocks he grew with seeds from Claude Monet's garden at Giverny, some of which I now have growing in my own garden. Dash stopped hanging out with my mother when she had me because, she gathered from things he said when drunk, he thought becoming a mother made her boring.

While Frank O'Hara liked children far more than most men on the scene did, he, too, parted ways with some women when they married or had children.

When Bunny Lang moved to Boston and married, O'Hara felt abandoned.

When Grace Hartigan moved to Baltimore and got married, LeSueur said, her analyst told her she should cut ties with O'Hara (and all her "neurotic" friends back in New York) to give the marriage a better chance. She wrote O'Hara a letter that hurt him deeply. He'd adored Hartigan, even tried to get her to go to bed with him, but she'd rejected him first sexually as a lover and now as a friend. He would give her future art shows scathing reviews.

When the artist Jane Freilicher got married, inherited some money from her mother, and had a daughter, O'Hara felt betrayed. "She's more interested in her new refrigerator than in her painting," Joe LeSueur told my father O'Hara had said. "He didn't like the way she got middle-class . . . He wanted it the way it was before, where you sit around and drink and talk and you weren't concerned about all that shit."

How often one person's liberation is another's subjugation. Second-generation New York School poet Alice Notley wrote:

> There is no place in America for heterosexual poets with children
> [. . .] except for
> in your house.

Chapter 14

I was over at my parents' place for dinner when I spotted a new novel by the art historian Irving Sandler called *Goodbye to Tenth Street*. Irving Sandler managed the Tanager Gallery on East Tenth Street in the 1950s and drank with the abstract expressionists at the Cedar Tavern. I flipped the book over and read the back. It was a novel set in the downtown art world from 1956 to 1962. O'Hara appeared in it as a character. I skimmed for his name and found him a third of the way into the book, at the Five Spot. Someone compliments a review he wrote about the abstract expressionist painter Franz Kline and he replies, "Gee, thanks."

Irving Sandler was one of the tapes I still had to listen to.

"Oh, hey!" I said to get my father's attention. He was reading a newspaper. "Can I borrow this Irving Sandler book?"

"No," he said. "I'm saving it for Spencer."

At least I had the Sandler tape.

Irving Sandler—6/3/77

Irving Sandler: Again, the thing I had mentioned was this absolutely fantastic concentration. Anyone he was with and talking to. You could be in a room with several hundred people. If Frank was talking to you, there was no one else there. Extraordinary. The other thing was this generosity. I mentioned that even before I had achieved any kind of recognition or reputation, Frank asked me to do a proposal and an early show of abstract expressionism that he not only presented at the Museum of Modern Art, which was quite extraordinary, but really tried to push.

Peter Schjeldahl: What year was that?

Oh my God! I shout at the tape recorder. *You do this every time! They're trying to share feelings and memories and you start grabbing for years! You're dragging them to the analytical, boring side of their brains like some kind of bohemian Joe Friday—"Just the facts, ma'am."*

My father also keeps interjecting his own opinions. It sounds like he's trying them on for size. "[O'Hara] is much more a creature of sentiment and soul," he tells Sandler. "He never went to a psychiatrist. He had nothing against it. I think he just never needed it. He was astoundingly nonneurotic. For being as unconventional as he was."

Sandler tells a long story about writing an *ARTnews* article in 1957 called "Mitchell Paints a Picture." And he recalls getting a statement from her for a piece titled "Is the Artist with or Against the Past?"

"Frank was sitting there while Joan was dictating her statement to me. We didn't have a tape recorder. Nobody used tapes then." When Sandler read Mitchell's words back to her, she got cold feet.

IS: Joan suddenly got very unsure about her answers and whether to let them go. She turned to Frank, and Frank just said very simply—I remember how simply and directly and how tough he was about it— he said, "Your answers are terrific. Don't change a word. Let it go." And Joan said, "That's it." And it was printed the way she said it.

PS: That sounds very characteristic. That would seem to be his—I think that was his basic piece of advice in every circumstance whatsoever, from poem to painting to love affair to whatever: *Go with your first impulse and you're terrific, do it!* Or else: *You're horrible, get lost!* [Laughs.]

IS: I have a feeling about Frank, that I half kept expecting him to say that to me: *Get lost.* I don't know why. There was a fastness about him that I never had. I always felt like I was stumbling when I was talking to him. I would really almost exaggerate certain—

PS: You felt intimidated by him?

IS: A little bit. Inadequate.

PS: You weren't quite interesting enough?

IS: Yeah! That I wasn't quite interesting enough. But also I would pull conversational gaffes almost that I normally wouldn't unless I was in a situation where . . .

PS: Out of an urge to become interesting, to him.

IS: Yeah.

I keep thinking about that phrase Sandler uses: "I wasn't quite interesting enough."

That's how I feel about my father: I've just never been that interesting to him.

Listening to his voice on the tape recorder, I realize he is in his midthirties, ten years younger than I am now, a new father, trying to do something he's never done before. But he can't maintain focus even in these one-hour interviews about his favorite writer.

I want him to be better. Why can't he just sit back and listen to these stories, gently guide them? Instead, he follows tangents, asks irrelevant questions, interrupts stories that are going well in order to nail down a timeline, causing his subjects to lose track of what they were saying. He keeps wanting to show off, when everyone knows the way you get good quotes is by playing dumb. He loses track because he's not paying attention.

PS: Let's see, what were we talking about?

Younger than the people he's speaking with, unsure of himself—he's not a version of my father I've ever considered before. I feel pity for him.

The truth is, he isn't suited to biography, which requires sustained curiosity about other people and their meaning to one another. His writing is about looking closely at art, which does not talk back, and then thinking about what he's seen. Neal describes it like this: "He not only doesn't see the forest for the trees; he's down on the ground with a magnifying glass."

My aunt Ann says my father told her: "I'm happiest when I'm talking and other people are listening."

Even though he is not doing a very good job of asking the right questions, I still feel like I'm getting to know O'Hara personally through these interviews. What I'm starting to see is how strangely spiritual O'Hara was while being so present in the world. He was witty and charming, and yet so much of what he wrote was about death.

Bill Berkson once said, "There is always some death in an 'I do this I do that' poem."

Helen Vendler wrote, "O'Hara was stubborn enough to wish, like Emily in *Our Town*, that life could always be lived on the very edge of loss, so that every instant would seem wistfully precious. Therefore the attitude of perpetual wonder, perpetual exclamation, perpetual naïveté. O'Hara had enough of all these qualities by nature (judging from their consistent presence from the earliest poems to the latest) so that this poise at the brink of life was no pose, but it does make me wonder how he would have endured that jadedness of age that, in their different ways, all poets confront."

This may be what I admire in O'Hara more than anything else: his "poise at the brink of life." One of my pen pals, the poet Sparrow, once told me that his daughter had made him see that Frank O'Hara had an enlightened, saintlike quality that often gets ignored: "We fail to recognize an elevated being simply because he's smoking a cigarette. God speaks through inebriated curators."

Chapter 15

One tape had an illegible name so I sent the audio to my father and asked if he could identify the voice. He wrote back later that day: "The painter Norman Bluhm, one of the better second-generation AbExers [abstract expressionists]. I liked him. Interview boring at first but tangy gossip later. He demobbed in Paris after the war. Cultivated air of a French tough guy. Appears in a scene of Cocteau's *Testament of Orpheus*. I'm vague about Frank's falling-out with Grace Hartigan, except it was dramatic. She moved to Baltimore."

Bluhm's voice is booming, hyperconfident. He sounds like a cop in a slapstick comedy. The Cedar Tavern painters scene was known to have a macho vibe, but this is the first time I can hear it so clearly. The level of confidence is staggering. Not a doubt in the world. Not a moment of hesitation. In his cold studio, Bluhm and O'Hara spent Sundays painting, writing, and listening to Sviatoslav Richter's version of Tchaikovsky's first concertos.

Norman Bluhm—1977?

Norman Bluhm: We used to talk about music. He used to come over. After a while he'd come over almost every Sunday. We'd play music and talk about it. Like those poem paintings—that's how they were formed, actually. Frank would come over on a Sunday, then we'd have lunch, go over to my studio, and we'd listen to the opera or to the symphony and we'd talk.

Then he tells stories about mocking people for being fat and stealing $80 from one of them at the Cedar. He recalls going uptown to art openings with O'Hara and some others on the night of the Cuban Missile Crisis in October of 1962. They stopped off for a drink at the Winslow Hotel and he loudly asked for "a neutral table." When a man at the bar objected, Bluhm made a crack about his weight and said it was obvious he wasn't ever in a war.

I'm prepared for the fact that Bluhm is going to share stories of O'Hara's sex life, because *everybody* seems to have stories about O'Hara's sex life.

NB: He was telling me one night about how some guy invited him up to an apartment, put him down on the bed, and started to fly above him on a trapeze or something like that. One of the wildest stories I ever heard in my life.

PS: My impression is that he sort of cooled the adventuring around fifty-six.

NB: Yes, but I think Frank used to tell me or certain friends of his, his adventures, in order that he could somehow vicariously get a hold of your adventures.

PS: He was avid for your adventures.

NB: Yeah. Oh, he loved it. Oh! He just loved that.

O'Hara's sex stories seem lighthearted—trapezes!—but there's a vulgarity to Bluhm's, an obsession with physical beauty and conquest.

I move on to Bluhm's more famous contemporary, Willem de Kooning.

My parents have a peculiar picture by de Kooning: oil on a sheet of the *New York Times*, from 1977. (You can make out just enough print to identify the paper's obituary of Woody Guthrie.) At the time, de Kooning kept the surfaces of his paintings in progress fresh by covering them with newsprint between sessions of work. My father tells me that on one of his visits to the artist, de Kooning said, "You shouldn't leave here with nothing." He kneeled and went through a pile of peeled-off sheets: "No. No. No good. No. Hey, this one's not bad. You like it?" He signed it in charcoal: "To Peter, Bill de Kooning."

The surface is alive with confident brushwork in blue, yellow, teal, pink, white. I knew it was valuable when people expressed horror that paint was sticking to the plastic front of the cheap frame. While over for a dinner party, the comedian Steve Martin and a collector friend insisted on paying to have it restored and reframed.

There's nothing figurative there, but one time when I was sick, half-asleep on the couch, and delirious, I looked at the dark blue lines in the picture and saw a man with a hat and a long arm pointing down. Every time I've looked at the picture since, I've seen this long-armed man.

My father once told me he remembered a party at Patsy Southgate's in the 1960s: "She lived next to de Kooning. There was a party that he didn't come to but that was going very late. I was standing near the kitchen and there was a knock on the kitchen door. The door opened and it was Joan Ward, who was de Kooning's mistress and the mother of his only child. And she was battered, beaten up, and somebody next to me said, 'Oh God, he's been at her again.' And I thought, *Oh my God, are we gonna call the police? Are a bunch of men gonna go over there? And I wanna tag along!* No. Ward said they'd run out of scotch, and she wanted a bottle. She got a bottle, and she went back. That was my first whiff of de Kooning."

I turn on the tape. From the start of the interview, de Kooning sounds drunk. His accent is strong. He gets to talking about the abstract expressionists' "Eighth Street Club"—the members-only artists group founded in 1949 that held lectures and Saturday-night dances to Fats Waller. Mondrian apparently liked to boogie-woogie.

My father tried to bring the interview back to O'Hara but didn't have much luck. De Kooning kept talking about the time they hosted Dylan Thomas or which artists didn't pay their club dues (Franz Kline!) or the time in 1951 that publisher John Myers carried Elaine de Kooning up five flights of stairs because she had her leg in a cast but still wanted to go to a party.

Willem de Kooning—Springs, New York—8/17/77

Willem de Kooning: Now, Frank O'Hara.

Peter Schjeldahl: He gave a lecture.

WdK: He gave a lecture but before he gave a lecture, he would have that voice of his, you know. He would amplify his ideas.

PS: What kind of thing would he say?

WdK: Fuck you! [Laughs.] Well, "Fuck you!" he says, but he was very much liked.

De Kooning goes on to talk about how once he went to O'Hara to talk about troubles he was having with a girlfriend. They went on a long walk, and O'Hara made him feel better. Later, de Kooning says, O'Hara needed someone to talk to about his own romances and he upbraided de Kooning for being a bad listener: "He reminded me that he was listening to me and so I was supposed to be listening to him!"

When de Kooning visited O'Hara on his deathbed in the little Fire Island hospital, O'Hara was as concerned with manners as ever. He said, "Bill! So nice!" as if they were about to have a cup of coffee together. He died before de Kooning had made it home.

A couple of times on the tape, there is a terrible *SLAM*. De Kooning explains the noise: birds have been flying into the clear windows of his studio.

My father seems distressed but ignores the slaughter. The interview goes on, and my father quotes a line I've heard him say often, one O'Hara used as the kicker of an as-told-to interview with Franz Kline in the *Evergreen Review*: "To be right is the most terrific personal state that nobody is interested in."

Well, I'm interested in it. And I think that these people with their bird murdering and their wife beating are not right at all.

So I'm already cross when I reach the most outrageous O'Hara friend of all: Larry Rivers.

My father seems excited for this one. After so many careful interview subjects, at last here's one who is the opposite of careful.

The painter Larry Rivers, born Irving Grossberg in the Bronx in 1923, did not hold back. Frank O'Hara loved Rivers, nicknamed "Libertine Larry." In one of several essays O'Hara wrote about Rivers, he described him as "an enigma, and fascinating."

My father told me that Rivers—full of energy, hypersexual, a little scary—represented New York City to O'Hara. O'Hara was a poet of the city, so of course he worshipped Rivers. My father evidently worshipped him, too, writing in the *New York Times* in 1979: "Larry Rivers is one of the most fascinating personalities of the last 30 years in art."

Rivers told my father that he was a mess when O'Hara, "this Irish, broken-nosed Anglo-Saxon from up there who just graduated from Harvard . . . comes waltzing into my life!"

Larry Rivers—East Village, New York City
(404 East Fourteenth Street)—3/31/77
Peter Schjeldahl: Want to start at the beginning?

Larry Rivers: Anything. Anywhere you want. You mean what, like how I met him?

PS: Yeah.

LR: A lot of this is probably not going to be so accurate, but I'll try.

The pair met, as is documented by both of them, at a party at John Ashbery's in 1950. Rivers was twenty-six, a jazz musician and painter, living at 77 St. Marks Place, below W. H. Auden in the same building, on my parents' block. Literary stars were at that party, like Delmore Schwartz and the crew from the *Partisan Review*. Their mutual friends had predicted that he and O'Hara would get along, and they did not disappoint.

LR: In the living room there were very long curtains. It was one of those old houses—like on Eleventh Street or Twelfth Street—in which the wall is a foot from the window, like a deep box and then there's a window. So the curtains actually left a foot for us to actually be in, eighteen inches. And we stayed behind the curtains kissing or something like that and acting like children. And then he sat on the bed in his sneakers and asked me to sort of sit on the bed with him. He seemed sort of exotic for me. . . . It was the beginning of [my] experimentation with homosexuality really. A lot.

PS: Had you been doing that before?

LR: I think so. But it never seemed as funny and confused with literature and things like that. Frank started to write poems about it. Finally, there was a night I think Arnold Weinstein, myself, John Ashbery, and Frank O'Hara ended up in bed and took a picture. It was like a boat. It wasn't like we were in bed. It was as if we were going on some trip. It had nothing to do with sex. But there we were. It was a joyous period.

PS: Was there a period it did have to do with sex?
LR: With Frank? Yeah!

The line O'Hara used on Rivers before they had their tryst behind the curtain was so innocent—but also so strategic—it takes my breath away: "Let's see what a kiss feels like."

The pair had an affair, but the passion was mostly one-sided. O'Hara often fell in love with straight, attached men. Around the same time that O'Hara was pursuing him, Rivers was having an affair with Jane Freilicher.

LR: It was like all mixed. It was, as I say, "experimentation." I also thought it was a certain ego thing of feeling like what a fantastic person I am if I can make it with a man, a woman, animals. I used to try it with everything. It was, I don't think it was that original a personality but maybe it was. It was all mixed up with the literature, with sex, with the new thing. I would sleep with him one night, go be with a girl the next night. But he was much more affected by it. It meant more to him. It meant one thing to me but his was more inclusive, like what one would call romantic, what you think is love, sexual desire and interest and the—
PS: He was in love with you.
LR: I think so. And wanted it to continue.
PS: He wanted you to be his boyfriend.
LR: Right! At the same time, he knew it was impossible. He wasn't that dumb. Even in his early twenties he was already brilliant that way. He knew that he had things for men who couldn't love men.

Later on the tape, Rivers describes trying to seduce his sisters' sixteen-year-old friends. He brags that he took one to the zoo and "tried to fuck her," then went and told Freilicher about it.

Maybe he's just making up stories, engaging in the downtown equivalent of locker-room banter, but I don't care. I don't like the way he talks.

This puts me at odds with pretty much everyone on the New York School scene. Here's the cultural critic John Gruen describing Rivers: "An intense, wiry, not particularly appetizing-looking young man, he exuded an incredible electricity, and a most seductive and potent sort of sexuality. One felt one could throw oneself into the gutter with Larry Rivers and emerge purified."

I feel repulsed by the things Rivers says and also by my father's failure to point out that it is not cool to speak rapturously about sex with teenage girls. I understand that the tranquilized fifties were oppressive and that an energetic rebellion was in order, particularly for those who wanted more from life than comfort. It's not lost on me that many wonderful people—even saintly Karen Koch—loved Rivers, so perhaps I'm judging him too harshly. But I also know what it's like to be a quiet child surrounded by loud adults determined to shock. And I know what it's like to be "taken to the zoo."

Rare is the child of bohemia who wasn't preyed upon by adults in one way or another. Making my way alone around the city, I was followed and flashed and rubbed-up-against more times than I could count. A babysitter's boyfriend molested me once when I was five. One of my parents' dinner guests always told me I had great legs. I took it as a compliment at the time. Now that my son is at the age that I was then, I can't imagine making a comment like that to his friends or finding it amusing if a dinner guest said something like that to him. When I was fourteen, one of my father's colleagues stared lasciviously across a lunch table at my adolescent body; I crossed my arms over my chest and studiously stared off into space as he and my father, oblivious to my discomfort, talked about art.

When I started kissing boys in middle school, at least it felt like I was in control. It turned out lascivious attention wasn't bad if it was coming from someone cute—and I found a lot of people cute. Maybe there's some truth to the cliché about girls who don't get enough attention from their fathers becoming promiscuous, or maybe I just did it because it was fun. I didn't fool around with any United Nations guards—that I know of—but my best friend, Asia, did once yell at me: "Stop sleeping with all my friends!"

When I was still in high school, I dated a man who was twenty-eight. I look back on the time I spent in his Alphabet City apartment with the bathtub in the kitchen while my less-bohemian classmates were playing extramural soccer, and I feel neither exploited nor thrilled by it. Those sorts of relationships were inevitable. We children of bohemia were older than our years—and the men of bohemia were younger than theirs.

LR: And then it used to get *la vie de bohème*. Frank would come over. So silly. This is a little later. I would, say, have taken a shot or something and I had one reaction: I'd vomit straight for thirty-two hours. How I could ever have continued . . . I practically started vomiting before I did it. I got so anxious about doing it. So I would start to think about vomiting. Then it would be quelled by the drug. Then I would be tranquilized. Well, Frank would either have had a night out or I'd tell him I didn't want to see him. He'd come up at like two in the morning, come up the steps drunk, bang his head on the stairs. I'd come out and get him. He'd have to take care of me because I was ill. The whole place was full of grapefruit rinds and plastic from sculptures. Instead of being music—*la vie de bohème* going on—it was all this shit laying out in the studio. Days and days and days of no cleaning up. Horrible.

He sounds like he's bragging when he describes a morning when he woke up, having taken heroin the night before, to an auctioneer trying to sell off his work while he was still in bed. His landlord had won an order against him. And he sounds approving when he says that all the stories you hear about Jackson Pollock are true, even the one about how he once went up to O'Hara at the Cedar Tavern and out of nowhere shouted in his face, "Faggot!" Rivers said, "When [Pollock] came in he would do something outrageous to every person there. I was known in the circle to be someone who took heroin, so he would make signs about pushing a needle into his arm. Or if a guy was gay he'd make an obscene sucking noise. He was so simple and clear—he was sort of funny."

Maybe you had to be there.

In November 1952, Freilicher began an affair with the artist Joe Hazan, whom she would go on to marry. After she returned from a weekend with Hazan, Rivers went to see her at her place on Eleventh Street and they spent the night together. In an act of childishness, he reset her clocks to make her think it was later than it was, so she'd wake up early, something she hated to do. Then he went back to his St. Marks Place apartment to get his drawing pad. When he returned to the Eleventh Street apartment, O'Hara—yet another rival for her attention—was there posing for her.

Rivers borrowed razor blades from Freilicher, saying he needed to sharpen his pencils, and headed to the Metropolitan Museum of Art to do some drawings. When he got back to his place from the Met, he began cleaning the windows, looking out onto a bleak day. Then he thought of the razor blades. He hacked away at his wrists with them, then panicked when he saw the blood on his sheets. He called O'Hara, who came over and bandaged him up.

A few hours later, the painter Fairfield Porter drove in from South-ampton and brought Rivers out to stay at his house for a couple of weeks. (The Porters were always flying to the rescue of their friends. They liked to joke that the poet James Schuyler came to dinner and stayed for eleven years.)

At the Porters' estate, Rivers sprawled across couches and read Proust and complained about Freilicher not coming to see him. He did not know that O'Hara had lied and told Freilicher that Rivers did not want to see her. In his rage and isolation, Rivers went out and painted *Washington Crossing the Delaware*, one of his most famous paintings.

Back in New York, Rivers spent two weeks living with O'Hara, who would make them dinner at night and then, some nights, climb into bed with Rivers.

In the late 1950s, Larry Rivers dated my father's eventual book agent, the famously beautiful redheaded editor Maxine Groffsky. Before opening her agency in the mid-1970s, Groffsky had served as the Paris editor of the *Paris Review* and, before that, as the model for Brenda Patimkin in Philip Roth's *Goodbye, Columbus*.

When I called her, Groffsky told me that she was "a square from New Jersey" when she met Larry Rivers and the downtown poets and painters. "Can you imagine falling into that world when graduating from college? *Alice in Wonderland*. The art, the energy and excitement and fun in that world—simply amazing."

She added that contrary to the "sensationally inaccurate account" published by John Gruen, who said Groffsky wanted to marry Rivers, Groffsky and Rivers were in the process of breaking up—after two years together, it was just time, she said—when, in 1960, he hired a young Welsh woman named Clarice Price as housekeeper. Rivers asked Groffsky to go to California with him and she said no. Price went instead, and that was that. Rivers married Price and they had two daughters.

Beginning in 1976, the year I was born and my father signed a contract for his O'Hara book, Rivers began making a film called *Growing*, for which he had his adolescent daughters appear topless. A decade ago, one of the daughters petitioned the Rivers foundation to destroy that film. Her request was denied. There's a line from a *Vanity Fair* article about the situation that has haunted me since I first read it. A board member of the Rivers foundation dismissed Rivers's daughter's request with this comment: "You know a major artist made this film, right?"

I look around at other children who grew up in the art world. Some moved out of the city as soon as they could and became, weirdly often, lawyers. Others stayed in their famous parents' world, and it did not always go well for them.

Lisa de Kooning dropped out of high school and hung out on St. Marks Place in the 1970s with the Hells Angels. Under odd circumstances, she died in 2012 at the age of fifty-six, a sculptor and mother of three. The *New York Times* story about it was headlined—repellently, I thought—HER FATHER'S DAUGHTER. The article depicts her life as both lonely and indulgent and describes her as having devoted herself to motherhood and to protecting her father's artistic legacy. It repeatedly calls her youngest daughter, an artist, Lily rather than Lucy. And it describes her father as loving her but not being cut out for responsible fatherhood.

I'm struggling to understand how my favorite O'Hara poem, the beautiful "To the Harbormaster," could be about someone as seemingly unworthy as Rivers. Maybe the times have just changed too much for me to see his appeal.

What's certain is that I was not expecting to find this much darkness in Frank O'Hara's story. One reason why I liked the idea of this project was that I'd get to think about cocktails and cigarettes, snow falling over Greenwich Village, paint-spattered lofts. The silver-toned image of a quiet city where spacious apartments could be rented for $50 a month and no one ever ran out of gin, and where, when Larry Rivers won $32,000 on *The $64,000 Question*, he went straight to the Cedar Tavern and bought everyone drinks. This was supposed to be a world where the witty banter never turned cruel, affairs ended in no hurt feelings, and intoxication left no hangover.

If I'm honest, as I'm listening to these tapes and trying to make something of them, it's not going great. On the days when I'm listening to interviews with men like Larry Rivers, I'm irritable and not fully present in my own life. I'm also bothered by the fact that I spend a lot more time thinking about them than I do about O'Hara's college lovers. Maybe it's true; maybe villains are more interesting, and the moral high ground does lack entertainment value.

As I walk around the city these days I'm walloped by memories of random people, places, and things from my own past: Ray's Pizza on Eleventh Street, where as fourth and fifth graders we could go out for lunch and where we dabbed with our paper napkins at the grease pooled on top of the hot cheese. The camel-colored wool coat with the big buttons I got at a thrift store when I was eighteen and wore until it fell apart. The Alphabet City studio apartment of a *SPIN* coworker where I used to housesit until he died of an overdose. Listening to those O'Hara tapes from the 1970s about the 1950s has me living somewhere other than the present. I keep hearing Rivers and Bluhm and de Kooning and my father even when they're not playing through my headphones. Their voices are loud inside my head.

Chapter 16

There weren't many children on the downtown scene of the 1950s and '60s, but I'm happy to discover that my father did find one to talk to. Born in Paris in 1953 to Patsy Southgate and author Peter Matthiessen, Lucas Matthiessen lived in New York with his mother and her new husband, Mike Goldberg, during the 1960s. In family friend Frank O'Hara Lucas discovered a third, more nurturing father figure.

Lucas Matthiessen—10/6/77

Lucas Matthiessen: Well, I remember particularly his presence. He was, as you probably know, around our house when I was a child a great deal of the time, particularly in the evenings. And I remember feeling very much a part of that world—very much one of the adults, so to speak.

Peter Schjeldahl: When were you born?

LM: I was born in 1953. I remember Frank as far back as when I was six or seven. I recall particularly how very, very warm he was towards— well, towards me especially—but towards children in general. As you probably also know, he really loved Larry Rivers's kids, too. And I think that this is very unusual for a New York homosexual poet, that

119

particular aspect of him. He was in many ways a sort of a surrogate father to me, in that—as you know my own parents were divorced when I was quite young. I was three, and Mike Goldberg spent a year in the nuthouse when I was twelve, right around the same time that Frank was killed. Also Mike, great pal that he is, had a certain sense of irresponsibility about him that Frank somehow made up for. This is not to say that Frank did not indeed display flightiness all the time, which he did, but there was a certain foundation about him, a certain security which I felt around him, which Mike did not possess. I remember especially a great deal of joking. We used to have great tomato and pear fights all the time. The two of us, we would each get a bucket of whatever rotten thing was lying around and whale away at each other. We even once contemplated watermelons, but then decided that neither of us wanted to risk a skull fracture.

PS: Would you go swimming with him at all?

LM: Oh yeah. There was a great deal of play in the ocean. I remember being tossed back and forth between Frank and Joe LeSueur all the time. We would ride waves together. Both of us were relatively fearless, I think, when it came to the water.

PS: Frank is legendary as a swimmer.

LM: Oh yes. So am I, actually. From a very young age I would plow into any surf and so would he. People would stand in awe, watching us disappear. I remember especially a sense of closeness toward him, which as a child now and talking about, I really don't think has been replaced, at least that particular kind of closeness.

Aside from one memory in which O'Hara called de Kooning's girlfriend Joan Ward a whore at John's Restaurant on Twelfth Street, Matthiessen remembers O'Hara as being in control of himself and never cruel, even when extremely drunk.

O'Hara gave the young Matthiessen life advice, read his writing—including a sixty-page story about a dog named Arf who lived in medieval times—and helped him with his homework. In a chaotic world, O'Hara was an anchor.

One time, Matthiessen's family spent the weekend at *Sophie's Choice* author William Styron's house in Connecticut. With Chubby Checker blaring, Styron boomed, "All we do in this house is twist and fuck!" Matthiessen says that remark summed up those years for him: the grown-ups around him all twisting and fucking their way through the Village and the Hamptons. When he was seven, he called his mother, to her face, "a beatnik nudist."

O'Hara told Matthiessen that autonomy would be important for him, that he shouldn't become a hanger-on or a junkie, as so many artists' children did.

> LM: Frank as poet meant nothing to me at that age. Nothing at all. Because everyone was a fucking poet or artist or something, you know. Everyone was creative, for Christ's sake. I really didn't place that much importance on it at the time. It was Frank's personality that mattered to me. Frank as friend, certainly.

O'Hara died when Matthiessen was only twelve—the same year he entered boarding school (which he hated), Goldberg had a mental breakdown, his mother started drinking even more heavily, and he had a miserable visit in Ireland with his father. The boy spent the day of the funeral looking around at the adults, feeling disgust.

Matthiessen remembers Larry Rivers delivering his famous graveside eulogy, in which he described O'Hara's bruised, broken body in the hospital room in great detail.

My father was at the funeral, but he went home to write up O'Hara's obituary for the *Village Voice* rather than attending the reception that followed. Matthiessen tells him what he missed.

LM: I remember Joe [LeSueur] crying hysterically, just almost out of control. I remember Allen Ginsberg and his trio of Moonies or whatever. They were doing their Zen mantra number. And [Ginsberg's partner] Peter Orlovsky . . . jerking off. Peter was jerking off.

PS: Where? In the house?

LM: On the deck outside. That was the first sense that I had of really how important Frank was. This is an indirect thing, but that the world didn't make sense without him. In other words, that the funeral, with Larry haranguing on and on about what Frank looked like in the hospital and the awful business and the whole deal. And Orlovsky jerking off. And Ginsberg playing his little flute or whatever the hell it was. It was like bedlam.

PS: Frank would have been the policeman and straightened everybody out.

LM: That's right. It's not so much he would have made sure—it wouldn't have happened with him. These people without him were just completely out of control somehow. There was no continuity. There was no—

PS: —center.

LM: Center. I was a child of twelve or thirteen, whatever I was when he died, but I remember feeling that very, very strongly—that this was just complete insanity.

PS: What else do you remember about the scene after the funeral?

LM: Well, everyone got very drunk. And I think what everyone was trying to do was to almost celebrate themselves. You know? That the ideal funeral was not to feel sorry for yourself but to give the dead a last drink or something, a last hurrah. But, Jesus, it certainly didn't work that way. You know, it was just complete craziness.

PS: Do you remember Frank's brother being there?

LM: I don't remember him being there. I remember Maureen being there.

PS: What do you remember about that?

LM: I've always had a crush on Maureen, from a very young age.

PS: She does *not* have a crush on me, by the way. I don't know if you've heard.

LM: I hadn't heard that rumor.

When I look up Matthiessen online I discover that he is the only person besides my father on any of these tapes who is still alive. According to the article I find, he's become a social worker. For me, he is the moral heart of these interviews, the voice of reason and gratitude, the defender of Frank O'Hara's—for lack of a better word—soul. I feel a kinship to him because in a far more roundabout way Frank O'Hara, as my father's role model, was a surrogate father figure for me, too.

Except that my father didn't copy this side of O'Hara's personality: his love of children. He saw the smoking, the drinking, the banter, the playfulness with language, but I don't think he saw past any of that to the spiritual grace that let O'Hara have food fights with children.

LM: Frank, you know, always did have this—I think I used the word "foundation" earlier about him—something secure, something solid, which none of these people, or very few of them, showed after he died. And really have yet to show. Because there was a— God, why do I keep using the word "moral"? The word "moral" keeps coming up and rings true. There was a certain morality, and there was a certain *dignity*. "Dignity" is the real word. Frank had more dignity than anyone else around him. And despite all the reports you're going to hear, in my opinion, of Frank's bitchiness and blah blah blah, I don't think that those people, that was the main lesson they didn't learn, that dignity was perhaps the most important thing: personal, individual integrity and adherence to one's own set of maxims or principles. PS: I think that's a good note to end on.

Chapter 17

My father got sober when I was sixteen. My mother threw him out and made rehab a condition of his return. I should have been happier that he stopped drinking. He finally started paying attention to me, but it was not the kind of attention I'd craved. I arrived home one evening from hanging out with Asia, and he demanded that I talk to him. He told me he thought I was doing drugs.

I wasn't—not at that moment, anyway. Asia and I had done all our heavy drinking and drug experimentation when we were fourteen and fifteen. Two years past that, I was smoking a cigarette or two a day and drinking a little on the weekends. And I wasn't trying to hide it. No one ever told me I couldn't do those things. My father had said I should try drugs but just not get addicted to them, which, good girl that I was, is exactly what I'd done.

When I wound up needing knee surgery that year, my father didn't visit. Looking for scrap paper when I was back home and convalescing, I came across a notebook in which my mother had drafted a letter trying to convince him to visit me at the hospital, so I'd know he cared.

He often tells the story of one conversation we had at the time in which he tried to get me to attend his rehab group with him and to start going on my own to Al-Anon meetings. I said I didn't have the problem so I shouldn't have to go sit on a folding chair in a basement and be punished for what he had done. Infuriated by his timing, I apparently said the following, a line he repeats often for company: "Let me get this straight—*now* you want to be my dad?"

I am definitely overly identifying with Lucas Matthiessen, because as soon as I hit Play on the interview with his stepfather, Mike Goldberg, I feel combative. I'm put off by the lack of humility in Goldberg's voice, even after he's had eighteen months of inpatient psychotherapy and another decade back out in the world.

My father clearly considers him a friend. I learn that he even went to stay with Goldberg for a week and a half after he split up with his first wife, Linda. And so he seems sorry for Goldberg that when pop art came in, abstract expressionists like him were passé.

"You must have had an ambition to become rich and famous?" my father says. "And it must have seemed in the late fifties inevitable that you would be? Or famous anyway?"

Goldberg says he's okay with his lack of fame, but he doesn't sound very convincing.

They critique the work of Grace Hartigan, who divorced her husband and sent her son to live with her in-laws in order to focus on her art. Hartigan was one of the only female painters on the scene who had a child. For a while, she showed under the name George Hartigan. In an oral history conducted by the Smithsonian, she said she hadn't seen her son since he was twelve, though now that he was in his midthirties, he'd sent her pictures of his three children. She hoped to meet them: "My oldest granddaughter, she looks like me. It's the grandkids I want, I don't want the son! [She laughs.]"

These people are the *worst*.

My father and Goldberg muse about who Gregory LaFayette— who shows up in a poem of O'Hara's—may have been. My father has asked around and come to the conclusion that he must be "some Cambridge person."

This is where living in the computer age gives me an advantage. I didn't get to drink at the Cedar Tavern, but I can look things up on IMDb. Gregory LaFayette was a blond actor who appeared in movies such as the 1957 war film *Under Fire*. He died in a car accident in Wyoming on the Fourth of July, 1957. His wife, Judy Tyler, had just filmed *Jailhouse Rock* with Elvis. The couple was driving back to New York with their cat and dog when they were in a head-on collision. The "other Gregory" of the poem was Beat poet Gregory Corso, whose intensity the two on the tape agree was more appealing when he was young.

Goldberg recalls O'Hara talking about the deaths of his grandfather and father. "That's something you should talk to Maureen about: *What is the first family death that you remember?* You see yourself in that. It's always scary."

That had actually never occurred to me before Goldberg said it. When our family members die, it's sad not only because we loved them but also because we see our own features drained of life. My father doesn't seem to register this insight from Goldberg, and he moves on to yet another question about sex.

My father's interview with Lucas Matthiessen's mother, Patsy Southgate, which I listen to next, offers some perspective on Goldberg. According to her, the reason he went into a mental hospital was because he was wanted by the FBI. He'd forged checks and paintings, and Southgate left him not only because of the criminal activity and lying but also because she began to suspect he was a sociopath: "I was bothered by what's known as a personality defect," she said to my father. "In his case, in matters of money, things like forging checks, stealing paintings, and forging signatures. Where you or I would get sweaty palms and increased heart rate, anxiety, Mike would experience nothing whatsoever."

Southgate was probably O'Hara's best friend toward the end of his life. O'Hara called her "the Grace Kelly of the New York School." She responded, "I don't think I was quite as uptight as Grace Kelly. But I was blond."

O'Hara confided in Southgate more, perhaps, than in anyone else. She recognized, behind the courtliness and the effusive conversation, a reserve. She said the drinking and the perfect manners were ways to hide that shyness: "When you're helping someone on with their coat, you don't have to talk to them," she said.

Southgate knew about his childhood, about his affairs, about his tough relationship with his family. She was there when his mother called, drunk and out of control, begging for money. He left those calls feeling terrible, she said, whether or not he gave her any.

When Goldberg and Southgate split up, O'Hara took Southgate's side, which I'm happy to hear. He was protective of her and her children, and he was angry about how poorly Goldberg treated them. O'Hara and Southgate began spending even more time together then. She saw how exhausted his increasingly challenging job at the museum made him. He was working more, writing less, and drinking an awful lot.

"He would finish off the vermouth in the morning if all the gin was gone before going to work," she said. "Or he'd put bourbon in his orange juice before going to the museum." As he neared forty, she suspected him of having something like a midlife crisis. "He was getting bald," she said. "He was combing his hair over, but his hair would blow away. He was very vain about his looks."

Patsy Southgate—New York City—9/22/77
Peter Schjeldahl: Did he talk about death much to you?

Patsy Southgate: Well, I think it was very romantic. As I say, we spent a great deal of our time late at night listening to opera, during which people *expired* . . . I think he had a romantic notion of death. I don't think he was at all suicidal—

PS: Absolutely not.

PSo: —or had any intention of doing himself in. As a matter of fact, he never laid any sort of depression on anybody.

PS: Except in terms of getting angry?

PSo: Umm-hmm. The only time I realized something about him was that after Mike and I split up, Frank and I went around together everywhere. He was living on Broadway across from Grace Church. I would come over to his place every night, and we would go do something. And I became aware— Often in that period, the museum would be sending him places like to Poland and to Spain, places like that where he didn't know anybody. He would be in an advanced state of panic about packing. He needed someone there to say, "Should I take the red tie or the black tie? How many pairs of socks should I bring?" As though he completely turned into a child at the prospect of leaving. I felt very able to help him in the role of being almost sisterly or motherly or wifely. That's the only time I saw him really seem needy or vulnerable or confused was prior to traveling.

When LeSueur moved out of the Broadway loft into an apartment near Second Street, at 26 Second Avenue, Southgate observed that O'Hara became frantically social. LeSueur hadn't liked very large crowds or very late nights and so he'd served as a kind of bouncer. When it was up to him, a fun night would consist of playing bridge, eating a good dinner, and going to sleep at a reasonable hour. Southgate became annoyed that now she had trouble getting through to O'Hara on the phone because his line was always busy, and he always seemed to be hanging out with Bill Berkson, whom she didn't love. Asked if she agrees with some others that "Bill was Frank's pet monster," she won't go that far but she does grant that "Bill was very possessive about Frank."

Southgate says what O'Hara really craved, out of everything, was companionship and love and even the comforts of family life. "I think human exchange recharged Frank's batteries," she says. "He'd have made a wonderful father. He was tireless in his patience."

Then she asks my father his age.

PSo: Being forty is a big one. Are you forty yet?

PS: I'm thirty-five.

PSo: When you hit forty, it's the worst birthday in the world.

PS: I haven't been bothered by birthdays since twenty-nine practically killed me. Ever since then it's sort of been easy.

PSo: You're too old to die young at forty. You can still die young.

PS: I don't want to die young. I just hope I can make forty in some style.

PSo: I'm sure you can. Anyway, I think it would be a mistake to try and read into Frank's life a desire to die.

PS: Oh, absolutely. I agree completely with that. It's completely unfounded. The contrary is true.

PSo: He had a great desire to live. Although there were a great many blows, and forty was a tough period, and Frank's life was in a certain turmoil, with a lot of tension, that's a part of life.

PS: Sure. In his case, that's something I'm going to have to unravel to my own satisfaction. What exactly were the factors? It's peculiar. If he'd gotten older, if he'd lived, it would have resolved one way or the other.

O'Hara didn't have a death wish, but at forty he was drinking an awful lot and throwing himself into the surf. I wonder if O'Hara is where my father got the idea that healthy lifestyles were for boring people, that it was cool to be cavalier about one's health.

"I don't bother my body and my body doesn't bother me!" he has always crowed.

But it was a lie. He smoked three packs of cigarettes a day from his teens on. He drank heavily until he was fifty. He never exercised, didn't take care of his teeth, and most mornings he would eat Entenmann's chocolate donuts or bacon for breakfast. I asked him to at least take vitamins, but he said he was suspicious of them. He seemed to believe that he could miraculously get whatever nutrition he needed from snacks of corned beef hash out of the can.

And his body bothered him right back. It had been decades since he'd been able to sleep without Ambien. He was weak and easily fatigued. He had almost none of his original teeth left. That he'd stayed relatively healthy for so long seemed to be more of a tribute to his parents' hearty Norwegian genes than to some internal deal he'd brokered.

Perhaps Frank O'Hara's death at forty, while he was still a strong swimmer and first-rate party guest, let my father believe that there would never be a reckoning. Cigarettes and drinking didn't kill O'Hara, and so maybe they wouldn't kill him either.

The winter Oliver was four, he refused to wrap his scarf around his neck. When I asked him why he said: "Poppa doesn't take care of himself, and I don't either!" I was relieved when a few years later, no longer enamored with my father, he chose instead to model his diet and exercise habits after those of my stepson, Blake, a physical therapy student with a black belt in kung fu.

> PS: I think I turned some kind of corner on this book. I'm starting to
> live with him.
> PSo: Oh good. He's a fun person to be with.

With that, my father said goodbye to Patsy Southgate and then put the tape recorder into his bag. But he unwittingly left it on. I listened to the sound of him walking through New York City, the tape player bouncing around in his bag: *scrumpf, scrumpf, scrumpf.* I expected to hear it switch off, but instead, a few minutes later, I heard his voice again.

Peter Schjeldahl: [A telephone booth door opens and shuts. A church bell chimes in the distance.] Hi! I just got out. I'm over by Fifth Avenue. What time is it? [It seems he's calling my mother.] Uh-huh. I'm over by Fifth Avenue. Would you . . . Let's see. I could come and pick you up and ring and we could go? Five thirty. I'll be there in about fifteen minutes? Okay. I'm going to buy a bottle of wine on the way. Did you get the mail? A letter from Maureen? I thought I mailed it yesterday. No, no. Because I talked to Joe LeSueur. He said Maureen had gotten my letter and mailed me one. Yeah. Well, I didn't know. I just talked to him now with Patsy. He said he'd been talking extensively to Maureen the last couple days and he wants to see me tomorrow. This thing has gotta be resolved. I don't know. He sounds supportive, yeah, of me. I don't know, though. I mean, it's so strange. But evidently Maureen is just . . . Yeah, well, I feel immune. I really do. Yeah. Okay. I'll talk to you in about fifteen minutes. Bye. Bye-bye. [Sound of the receiver being replaced and the telephone booth door opening. Chimes get louder.]

Listening to this call, which I am probably the only person to ever hear since it was recorded, I think of how reliant he's always been on my mother. He was fifteen minutes from home but still had to call her. I can't hear her end of the call, but I can imagine her reassuring him, calming him, encouraging him.

Where would my father have been without her? She cooked his meals, raised his daughter, cleaned his house, kept their social calendar, and most years made more money than he did at the same time. She rearranged the furniture, set out flowers, rotated in holiday decorations. She did it all very well. The best hosts make everything, from the couch's slipcovers to the meringue dessert, seem like no trouble at all.

She's always had a gift for painting, and sometimes she'd get out her basket of acrylic paints and cover trays, walls, and lampshades with intricate floral patterns. But no one ever took it seriously. Once when I encouraged her to make more space for herself in the apartment, she said she was fine with her little table by the window in the living room, where she also balanced their checkbook and paid their bills.

Why was he still considered the head of the household? Why was he the genius who needed all that time and space? You don't see many women baffled about why history lacks more women artists or novelists or stand-up comics. How dare anyone say that an entire group of people aren't funny if for millennia they aren't allowed to try writing jokes until they've done all your laundry, cooked all your food, and put your children to bed?

My friend Abbott says women who want to create anything need to train themselves to be 10 percent more narcissistic. You need the extra edge of not caring, of self-assurance, of giving yourself permission to take up space. If your whole life you're told by the world to be quiet, to be small, to be pleasing, how do you override all those messages and go a different way? I read male memoirists with thousands of pages of stories and thoughts, and I don't know how they do it. And I wonder if I want to be like that or if I'm just intoxicated by how free they seem to feel.

I've spent decades hitting my assigned word counts and quoting other people at length, standing back from the text so as not to get in the way of my research. But where has that gotten me? My father's the star. I'm the good girl.

Beastie Boy Adam Horovitz—a poet of my generation and fellow graduate of PS 41—once told me that the age requirement for drinking on St. Marks Place was "confidence." Maybe that's the age requirement for everything.

Chapter 18

One day around my grandmother's birthday, my father, Neal, Oliver, and I went to visit her at her assisted-living home. My father's mother, Charlene Schjeldahl, was turning 102, but her mind was as sharp as ever. For the year prior, I'd tried to bring or mail her at least a book every month. Reading had become her main activity aside from playing Scrabble with my aunt Peggy or working the *Daily Star* crossword puzzle with my aunt Ann and cousin Mary Ann (Grammy often finished it first). On one visit, she'd recited Emily Dickinson's "'Hope' is the thing with feathers" to me from memory.

On this trip, I brought her donuts, a book by Roz Chast, a Norway guidebook, and Tommy Orange's *There There*, because she'd recently become interested in Native American literature. My father did not bring her anything, and he did not talk loud enough for her to hear him, so she mostly just smiled at him as he talked and then said, "What?"

Soon, my grandmother and father had stopped trying to converse and were in opposite corners reading to themselves—he Roz Chast and she the Norway guidebook.

Finally, I said, "We should get going." My father leapt out of his chair like he was a surgeon and a donor organ had just been located.

At various points, he has been estranged from each of his four siblings, and he has never forgiven his mother for her lack of warmth when he was young. In my father's defense, I know that people are often very different as grandparents than as parents, that it's entirely possible that Grammy had been a monster to him and an angel to me. Still, she seemed so eager to be close to all of us now, and she was so loving with Oliver.

"C'mon," I said in the elevator to my sulking father. "Grammy's a hundred and two! You're seventy-seven! And she's apologized! Can't you cut her any slack?"

"You weren't raised by her," he said.

No, I was raised by you. I thought back: my father driving into a boulder and almost killing us because he wouldn't listen to everyone in the car saying that it was too icy to take the shortcut; stranding Oliver at age ten alone at a town pool the one time he was put in charge of him; putting me on a city bus to go to a birthday party at age eight without quite telling me where the party was. I must have looked like an Edward Gorey cartoon standing there in the West Village in my party dress, holding a present, lost.

I always wished that when I was young he'd just picked, once and for all, whether to be smart and thoughtful *or* arrogant and callous. Instead, he'd be one thing for a week or two and then, without warning, the other. Unlike Grammy, he'd never changed. As a grandfather, he ran alternately warm and scalding, just as he had as a father.

Once, when he went to a war museum, he brought Oliver back a reproduction army satchel, a bull's-eye souvenir that Oliver carried with him to the playground for years. But when on a bright summer afternoon Oliver raved to him about how much he loved *To Kill a Mockingbird*, my father shut him down, saying, "It's no *Huckleberry Finn*." (Neal and I now use this phrase all the time. Dinner tonight? It was fine, but no *Huckleberry Finn*.)

Earning my father's approval has never been straightforward. One time I went to St. Marks Place to retrieve a spare copy of my Brooklyn keys because I'd locked myself out of my apartment. He'd lost many keys, wallets, and passports over the years and seemed delighted that I'd shown myself capable of such a blunder. As I trudged up the stairs, I heard him shout down the stairwell, "You are my daughter after all!"

This is why as a little girl I felt pride in my bad handwriting. My father's illegible scrawl was legendary, and I copied it. I found an old report card from elementary school: nearly perfect grades, all "Excellent," except for handwriting: "Satisfactory."

Starting when I was thirteen, I worked—at the farmers' market, as a babysitter, at the local comic book store. My parents spent most of every summer in the Catskills, leaving me alone in the apartment for months at a time starting when I was fourteen. I wanted them to go. I preferred the company of my friends.

My best friend, Asia Wong, stayed over for a few weeks that first summer. We both had jobs and took classes and drank and smoked but spent most of our nights walking around the city for hours. We had long discussions about, for example, which of us was Barbara Hershey in *Beaches* and which was Bette Midler ("No, I'm the wind beneath *your* wings!") while ignoring NYU students who were trying to pick us up.

The night before I was to start high school, I was in the apartment making myself buttered noodles for dinner, and I felt suddenly, horribly alone. Asia was home with her family. My parents were a three-hour drive away. I'd been acting like a grown-up for years, but that night I felt very young and very scared. I cried until I was almost sick, wrote Sylvia Plath–inflected poetry about suicide, and pondered methods for a couple of hours. Then, eventually, I pulled myself together and went to sleep. I got myself to my new school the next morning on time.

That year I started hanging around, like a stray dog, the family of some kids I babysat. They were part of the same New York intellectual class as my parents, but to me their relative domesticity made them seem unbelievably exotic. There were three children. Their mother put her kids' clothes in the dryer on winter mornings so when they woke up—to a tape of Beatles songs—they wouldn't have to put on cold shirts. The father was a journalist, writing stories about exciting topics like dinosaur bones, boxing, and drugs. He often brought his family on reporting trips. All through high school I slept at their house in Brooklyn twice a week so I could babysit at night and then take the kids to school in the morning.

By the time I was sixteen, I was babysitting for them and other families and working as an intern at *SPIN* and *Esquire*. I also tech-directed school plays and had a boyfriend. I barely saw my parents at all.

As a teenager and into my twenties, I did hold out hope that I would eventually receive from my father what I'd heard called an amends—a specific apology for things he'd done and left undone. I thought that if he sat down and made a long list of things he felt sorry about, then I could forgive him and we could move on. When I asked him, years later, why he had never made an amends to me, he said there was something you could do called "a living amends," where you just started living in a new way. I thought that sounded like a cop-out.

In my twenties, I decided I could just go ahead and make his amends for him. I could look into his heart and see that he wished he'd been a better father. I could become a ventriloquist, whispering consoling words to myself.

That strategy helped me, but nothing seemed to help him. He appeared sad and anxious. I once told him he should try to write about his life. I've taught memoir seminars, at which I always express my belief that if you tell a story in an honest enough way, you can free yourself from shame. He said he could never write a memoir because his memories were like a train yard full of third rails.

My mother says my father opens doors and drawers but never closes them. She's always following behind him, closing things. She's been complaining about it for fifty years. Still, she does it, because she doesn't want to live in a home full of open cabinet doors and gaping drawers. When I found these O'Hara tapes, I saw an open drawer. The past year it's like I've been trying to close it. Or perhaps I am just flinging open more drawers and cabinet doors—searching them for answers to questions about who my father is, who Frank O'Hara was, why people liked Larry Rivers so much, and how I can wring a happy ending out of all this.

Chapter 19

On February 13, a bit more than a month after my first overture to her, I received a message from Maureen. My heart leapt. She wrote:

Dear Ada,

Thank you for your journalist inquiry. I appreciated reading about your interest in Frank. I would like to talk with you. However, I would not like to be interviewed, as you suggested. Biography is not a good idea.

Although the interviews Peter recorded with Frank's friends were never shared with me, it would be important to think about publishing them if they are interesting.

I have a question. What has your father said to you about what happened when he and Maxine Groffsky, his agent, proceeded regarding a biography of Frank that did not work out at HarperCollins? Also, did your parents ever say that you were with them when they visited with me to talk about Frank here at my home? We were happy to greet you three.

Best wishes and congratulations regarding your lively, very interesting books, St. Marks Is Dead and Wedding Toasts I'll Never Give, and all the great reviews. I have enjoyed both books.

Congratulations to Peter regarding the collection of his art writings that will be published by Abrams in 2019.

Thank you for sending more details about your book idea. I look forward to hearing from you.

Sincerely,
Maureen

The email confused me. On one hand, it seemed warm and promising. On the other, there were red flags. I read and reread the line about how biography was "not a good idea." Did she mean in this instance or in general? If the latter, I wondered who would break the news to Ron Chernow.

I decided I should find some more people who knew her and could help me understand what she meant, so I reached out to the poet Vincent Katz. Katz had just asked my father to read at the Readings in Contemporary Poetry series he ran at Dia Chelsea.

At Le Pain Quotidien in Chelsea I found Katz still to be the sunken-eyed dreamboat who took me to *The Nutcracker* when I was five and he was twenty. I talked about the project and said I'd heard about a number of books Maureen had effectively killed, noting that she seemed to mostly only give permission to academic and small-press projects.

He said I should get to know her. I assured him I was trying.

When I asked Katz for his thoughts on Frank O'Hara he said, "God. He's God to me. He's just so good. Every time I think about him or read his work, it's just so inspiring. I mean, I could go on for days and days. I'll just say that I was reading your dad's poems out loud. I like to read poems out loud. And I came to 'To the Art Profession,' one of his later poems, and there's this one bit where he starts to do one-liners on contemporary critics. I said, 'Oh my God. He's doing a riff on Frank O'Hara's "To the Film Industry in

Crisis"!' So, I pulled that out and I read that and then I went back to Peter's poem."

Katz met O'Hara when he was a little boy: "My parents—probably you had this experience, too—if they were going to parties, they would take me most of the time. I remember at a party at his loft on Broadway I looked up and I saw him, and he said, 'Oh, he's just a bag of shit!' That was one of his favorite expressions. It was just so vivid that it imprinted on my memory. Then I said to my mom, apparently, 'I'd like to invite someone to dinner.' I was six. And she said, 'Who would you like to invite?' And I said, 'Frank O'Hara.'

"The last time my mother saw him, he was wearing this little button of James Dean and he took it off and he gave it to her. James Dean was very important to him. He wrote those three very memorable poems when James Dean died. To do that to me seems so generous. It's a generosity of spirit: 'I love this thing and here, why don't you take it.' That's him as a person."

Katz adored his parents' friends: "[New York School poet] Kenward Elmslie once played this game with me where he put this piece of paper in the typewriter and said, 'Whatever you say, I'm going to type.' And I said something like, 'What do you mean?' And he typed, 'What do you mean?' He didn't say anything else—so I realized I had to play the game."

When Katz was a teenager, he found poets as glamorous as rock stars. "Like that whole crowd, from your dad to Ted Berrigan to Anne Waldman—I knew them and they were friendly to me. I just loved the way they dressed and their poetry and seeing their attitude toward life."

This was not my experience. When I was young, I had no love for my parents' art-world orbit. Sometimes people hear that I grew up on St. Marks Place around famous artists and imagine it was like Paris in the twenties. And it might have been glamorous, but I didn't see it that way. I wanted to travel, to do things that felt important and Real. (As a teenager, I was prone to capitalizing words like "Real.") If anyone asked me what I wanted to be when I grew up, my typical answer was farmer, because that was the most tangible, least cosmopolitan option I could think of.

I asked Katz how he felt about the fact that these people were so famous at the St. Mark's Poetry Project but largely unknown outside of it. He said that's a problem for poetry in general: "There's a lot of energy but it doesn't seep out into the general culture as much. But it can. Bill Berkson talked about that and used the word 'seep.' He used the image of a leeching field. [Poetry] goes out into the culture, not always on the surface. It's not always that you're reading an article about it in the *Times* or the *New York Review of Books*, but it's somehow getting out there and affecting things."

I asked him what he thought of my father's poetry. He said, "I think he's really one of the best poets, honestly, of the generation. He should write poetry again. He should come back."

I mentioned a term I'd learned: "postulator," an investigator in the Catholic Church who builds a case for someone to be sainted. I told him that in this case maybe that's what I should be to Frank O'Hara, rather than his biographer.

Katz didn't think so. "I'm not sure if that needs to be done. I always think: *What is my ideal readership or viewership for this particular thing?* I always think of a specific person. My wife's a filmmaker. We worked on a documentary together once. I thought of a woman I know who's the editor of a Swiss art magazine: *If she likes this film, then it's going to be good.* If you want to reach a much broader audience, I could see that, but I'm thinking maybe you want to make it more about yourself. It's a great project. You can make use of the tapes and have a conversation with your dad, too."

Given the choice, is it better to write for a tiny audience of like-minded people or for a mass audience of strangers? I think most East

143

Village bohemians would say the former—that their aesthetic was only meant to be understood by a select few, including some who haven't been born yet.

In college I took advanced Sanskrit; my thesis was a translation from the Atharvaveda. I chose the course because I loved the Upanishads and wanted to read them in the original, because I loved dictionaries and grammar and Sanskrit had so many and so much of both, and because I didn't want to be compared with my father, to be called a chip off the old block, as if he were a monolith and I a tiny shard. If that meant I had to hide out in academia, I was okay with that. I was with Vincent: it's okay if you have a small audience if it's the right audience.

A Sanskritist friend of mine at the University of Chicago with whom I have a weekly online Vedic translation club emailed me a verse from an eighth-century play. She said it made her laugh because it epitomized the fantasy to which writers of every era cling, from Thucydides to the debut novelist whose book is remaindered.

ये नाम केचिदिह नः प्रथयन्त्यवज्ञां
जानन्ति ते किमपि तान् प्रति नैष यत्नः ।
उत्पत्स्यते तु मम कोऽपि समानधर्मा
कालो ह्ययं निरवधिर्विपुला च पृथ्वी ॥

Those, whosoever they are, who show disdain for us,
What do they know? This effort is not directed toward them.
Anyhow, some person simpatico to me will arise,
For time is boundless and the earth is wide.

At Dia Chelsea the day after our coffee date, Vincent Katz gave my father a glowing introduction, calling him a smart and funny member of the second-generation New York School and displaying an incredible grasp on the history of my father's poetry output. He appeared proud that he had wrangled my father into giving his first poetry reading in more than thirty years.

Vincent Katz—Dia, Chelsea, New York City
(124 Seventh Avenue)—3/5/19
Vincent Katz: Peter Schjeldahl's poetry keeps reminding me how poetry and life are inextricably intertwined—for everyone, although only some are aware of it.

Katz said his favorite of my father's poems was the surprisingly tender "On Cocksucking." No doubt disappointing the crowd, my father did not read that poem, nor any others that Katz referenced. He read only one poem, "Challenger Elegy," the last he wrote in verse, on January 29, 1986, and one he told me my book about Generation X reminded him of. I felt proud to have inspired its resurrection.

Dia—Chelsea, New York City (537 West Twenty-Second Street)—3/5/19
PS:
8.
I am here to say that I loved my teachers
A couple of them, anyway
And have been ungratefully forgetful
I am here to state
That father driving the station wagon pleased me in ways
That I am now only dimly aware of
Though it wouldn't have killed him to stop now and then
I refer to the goodness in going
Even if nowhere special
Of a nice, vague sensation of momentum
When someone you trust drives
A feeling that you can't remember the start of

And can't imagine ending
And should it go out in a cupola of flames, say?
It couldn't help but continue
Cradled in unknowing
As even now it continues
Father at the wheel
And the sky, so blue

After reading the poem, he read a medley of art columns from his forthcoming book with "the brilliant Spencer, who couldn't be here tonight."

Another night, not long after, my father read at the Strand from his new book of collected art criticism. Spencer interviewed him onstage and they discussed, among other things, how much Frank O'Hara had influenced his work.

After the event, keeping in mind what Spencer had said to my father about how I didn't seem to like his friends, I tried hard to be extra friendly to Spencer. I mentioned trying to do something with the Frank O'Hara tapes I'd found. Spencer recommended that I read Janet Malcolm's *The Silent Woman*. I thanked him for the suggestion and bought the book.

Malcolm writes that we do not own the facts of our own lives: "The ownership passes out of our hands at birth, at the moment we are first observed . . . Our business is everybody's business, should anybody wish to make it so . . . The biographer at work, indeed, is like the professional burglar, breaking into a house, rifling through certain drawers that he has good reason to think contain the jewelry and money, and triumphantly bearing his loot away."

If that's true, it would make sense that Maureen would want to bar the doors to my father, to me, and to everyone else. But I don't think every biographer is like a thief in the night. There are so many different ways to tell the story of a person's life, to do what Virginia Woolf called life-writing. I think of what Elaine de Kooning said of her faceless 1962 portrait of O'Hara: "When I painted Frank O'Hara, Frank was standing there. First, I painted the whole structure of his face; then I wiped out the face, and when the face was gone, it was more Frank than when the face was there."

I emailed Josh about the Maureen email and he said that, again, this all seemed promising. He predicted that over time she would come around and I'd have her cooperation, which would let me quote from his poetry and letters.

I wrote a note back to Maureen and told her that I was planning to drive up to Connecticut soon to visit the archives at the University of Connecticut, which contained some Frank O'Hara material. I asked if I could take her out for lunch when I was there.

I decided that when I went, I would bring her an early copy of my Generation X book and my father's new book and some New York City delicacies. Maybe rugelach. I would arrive right on time with my tape recorder and my notebooks—and my best manners. When she inevitably gave me permission to quote from O'Hara's work, it would be a lesson to my father about the right way to get things done, with diligence, deference, and professionalism.

Weeks passed and she did not respond. At the end of April, I decided it was time to schedule the O'Hara research trip, so I wrote Maureen again:

I hope you've been well! I will be visiting the University of Connecticut library next month, May 14 and 15. Would it be possible for me to take you out for a coffee or lunch either of those days? I would love to see you again—forty years since the last time I was there!"

The next day she called to give me her answer.

Chapter 20

Tuesday afternoon. I was working in a little basement office space I'd rented for a few months because I'd taken on two big ghostwriting projects at the same time. It was my first office with a door ever, and I loved it even though it was tiny, the walls were glass, and I was surrounded by tech bros yelling into headsets.

When the phone rang, I knew it was Maureen because I had her number saved.

This is it! I thought when I saw her name come up on my phone. *It's all happening!*

I grabbed a pen, planning to write down her address and the time and place we'd be meeting in May. But she was not calling to schedule a meeting.

As she spoke, I wrote down everything she said. I've been taking shorthand notes as a professional reporter for more than twenty years, so I'm confident in the accuracy of my transcription. As she knew I was a journalist investigating my father's book project, she never asked to go off the record, and this seemed likely to be her only comment on the matter. I present our conversation with only minor edits for clarity.

Maureen Granville-Smith: You wrote and said you'll be in Connecticut and you'd like to meet. I'd love to meet you, of course, but I do not support this project. I do not really think it is a good idea. I think it's great that you want to write about your father, but I think it's not a good idea to bring Frank into it. Frank really doesn't have anything to do with it. You have no idea what you're getting into. You probably know Maxine Groffsky.

Ada Calhoun: No.

MG-S: Well, she and your father . . . Your dad has all these wonderful things going on in his life. He has this book coming out. He's done this reading at Dia. If he didn't tell you what happened . . . Everybody was enthusiastic about his book at first. My feeling is that when people do a project, they need to use their strengths. You mention that some projects haven't happened. I expect one of those people was Amei Wallach.

AC: Yes.

MG-S: She is a wonderful person and art writer. She wanted to do a biography of Frank. She couldn't write about his poetry. She thought of him in terms of F. Scott Fitzgerald—Zelda, drinking, blah blah blah. That tells you everything you need to know. Biography is a subject where people need to know what they're talking about. When your father and mother came here, you were with them. You were just a baby. Peter was antagonistic, which surprised me. Frank liked his poetry, and I liked his poetry. He said all these things. Maxine Groffsky called me and told me they wanted access to the letters and all these things for five years and not to let others use them. Well, I said, "Look, I'm not in a position to grant those rights." There were already other publishers doing various things. They also wanted no usage fee. I thought it was preposterous, especially coming from a friend of Frank's, which Maxine was. They obviously had an agreement with Harper. You think you're dealing with friends and you're not. They asked another publisher who had the letters if they could see them, without even asking me! Well, of course that publisher called me right away. That was it. You have to understand this about Frank O'Hara: his legacy is fine. He doesn't need any help from you. Ada, you have all these wonderful books. Your career is going so well. You have to be very careful.

You love your father. It's a mistake to bring Frank into it. It's enough that I lost my brother the way he died. It's worse when people treat his work in this way. I cannot go along with anything that would treat Frank this way. Your dad when he was here was very antagonistic. I was very happy to have him here, of course. We talked and I told him about Frank and how good he was to me. I told him about all the books he gave me.

"He was controlling, wasn't he?" your father asked.

He was young. I just laughed, and I said, "No, Peter. He was a very loving person. He loved to share."

Peter said his relationship with women was a cover for his own sexuality.

I said, "No, no, no."

Another thing he said was that Frank wasn't a great poet. He said that John Ashbery was a much better poet. I started to laugh. I said, "I'm not in the ranking business."

He said he didn't think Frank was a great art writer. I said, "Why do a book about him, then?"

"Because he was an important art world figure," your father said.

You have no idea, do you? . . . You're so young. You have so many good things going for you. You don't want to dredge up a past that's not attractive. I was surprised you wrote to me as if you didn't know me. I can understand if Peter wants to publish his interviews. Why do a biography?

AC: I'm troubled that not everyone knows about O'Hara. I think more people should know about him.

MG-S: The trouble with Brad [Gooch]'s book [*City Poet*] is that he's very accurate in many ways but if you don't know what you're talking about, you can't do a good job. I knew him since he was an undergraduate. It's not really a biography. It's a hearsay book. Wasn't his life interesting enough without that? I came to New York. I worked at the Met, at the Guggenheim. I met Frank's friends. Frank was such a sharing, wonderful person. I knew who he loved the most. I won't tolerate gossip about him.

I hated the [2018 Mark Dery] biography of Ted Gorey [*Born to be Posthumous*]. It's people who didn't know him writing about him. I would caution you. You are young. You don't want to get into all this. All the people you listed who you want to interview—it's all hearsay. When I saw the draft of Brad's book, I was appalled. He sensationalized Frank's life. I tried to talk to Brad. I thought he should have gone to John [Ashbery], Kenneth [Koch], so they could see it and comment. I said, "Because you know they will comment afterward." I said to Brad, "You started out the book with the funeral service. It was exaggerated. You slap people in the face doing that. Young people reading it will never get a chance to really know him."

Peter wrote a piece in the *Village Voice*. That was good—it was *okay*, but he said he was on the decline in the last year. It's not true. When you get that out there—that he drank a lot, he wasn't writing, it's not true. He was not unhappy. He'd done [MoMA catalogs for] David Smith, Nakian. He was excited to have the summer off. I'm his sister. I knew. People say, publishers say, "You're just his sister." One publisher said, "You wouldn't like anything any writer wrote about your brother." That's not true.

Brad [Gooch]'s partner, Howard [Brookner], was dying of AIDS. When he slapped Frank, it seemed sad. I'm very respectful of people. Brad said, "Now the daggers are coming my way."

Frank did not have a miserable childhood. He had wonderful friendships when he was young. Being Catholic was different then. Being "over-parochialized" was how he put it, which was funny. Barbara Guest and all those poets were such individuals and so supportive of one another.

I'm distressed for Peter. It's nothing to me, of course. I wouldn't want this ugliness dredged up. I had no choice but to say no. I have nothing to do with any of it.

Ada, you have so many good things going for you. Now I hear you want to read the letters. You're going to go to the University of Connecticut. What does it have to do with Peter and Maxine? If you want to write about your father, write about your father. Don't bring Frank into it.

AC: I respect your feelings. I understand that—

MG-S: Do you? If you respect my feelings, you won't do this. But you've already interviewed people. I've heard about it from other people.

AC: Yes. I told you in my email to you, I've talked to a few people, but—

MG-S: I do not support the project. You sent me a "journalist query." What is that? I thought, *I'm Frank's sister! I don't want to be interviewed!* Frank had a wonderful life. I loved Joe LeSueur. Frank always said, "You are going to be so unhappy when Joe and I aren't living together anymore." But Joe got mean when he got older. No one likes to be in a position to say no, but . . . You're a journalist. You've written personal things about your life. You have your life ahead of you. I liked your book *St. Marks Is Dead*, but I saw in the description of the book, "Frank O'Hara caroused. Emma Goldman plotted." What was that? That is the kind of thing I am talking about. He did not carouse.

AC: I didn't write that. The publisher did. That's just part of a long description of the book.

MG-S: You seem confident, but you don't know that much about poetry or about music. In your letter to me, you're telling me it changed your father's life when he didn't finish the book . . . I would write about your father, but don't bring Frank into it. Play to your strengths.

AC: I hope I will prove your suspicions wrong. I want more people to know about Frank O'Hara. I think it's sad that he's so great and a lot of people have never heard of him.

MG-S: No, they do know him! People know him through his work! He was glad that he was known through his work. It's a preposterous idea that you're going to create some false construct of him. As George Montgomery said, "Don't lionize people."

AC: If you are worried that I will get it wrong, perhaps you can tell me how to construct one that's truer to life.

MG-S: I got from your letter that you want to do a biography, but you don't know enough about anything Frank cared about. Frank was an intellectual. It's not good to make someone into a character. You don't understand him.

AC: Well, I'm not coming at it as an expert but as a fan. He was my dad's favorite writer, and he is mine—

MG-S: No he wasn't!

AC: I know my father said something dumb when he was with you. He is kind of famous for putting his foot in his mouth, and I'm sorry about that. He misspoke.

MG-S: That's called misspeaking?! Everybody has always liked Peter and your mom. Peter didn't stop writing poetry because of this book. You are not in New York because of Frank. Your father didn't move there because of Frank. You are not on this earth because of Frank. You're saying, "I'm going to make things right." Why? You have this book on Gen X coming out. You've written about your life. I don't think you're up for this. What do you know about the composers

Frank admired? [She starts talking fast now; I didn't get all of it.] He was just terrific. You don't want to make a false character.

AC: No. Perhaps you could help me by telling me what other people have done wrong.

MG-S: I don't want to help you! Your writing is interesting, but that is not enough. Another writer who wanted to do a book about Frank couldn't write about art, only about theater. That's why Marjorie Perloff was good to work with. That's her field. She does understand the poetry. [Call got dropped, probably because I'm in the basement. I called back and she answered.] That was the phone telling me I've talked too long. I wish you all the very best. You can always contact me. You've taken on an ambitious project.

AC: I understand that.

MG-S: I don't think you understand! Do you? Do you think I will be allowed to listen to the tapes? Ada, you say your parents didn't tell you what was going on. You wrote to me and inferred that it was my fault, that I was *difficult*. I know what Peter said about me. I never went around badmouthing him. When John Ashbery asked me about the ordeal, I said, "I like to avoid painful situations." He said, "I like to avoid painful situations, too," and he laughed, because he understood what I meant. Frank died fifty years ago. I can't believe it. You say you want to finish a story your father didn't finish. I still don't know what story he wanted to finish. I don't know what else he wanted. I've written things down. I write everything down.

The Joe LeSueur business. FSG wanted to add Frank's poems to the book. They exploited him. Joe was very mean. And now Frank gets to be the mean guy? I know Frank made remarks people didn't always like. I was close to people he worked with at the Museum of Modern Art.

I would tread lightly. You are young. You have your whole life ahead of you. You have a child. I've never heard a word of apology from your dad or Maxine. They tried to take advantage of Frank! I did nothing to Peter. This is so silly. I'm talking about not getting into something you're not up for. You think you can go to someone and talk to them and you'll get a sense of the *Odes*? When I got your letter, I thought, *Oh my God, her parents didn't tell her.*

AC: I'm sorry you don't think I can do a good job with my idea. I'm disappointed to hear you don't trust me to do a good job.

MG-S: I trust in your writing. I don't think this will be a good project. Josh Schneid—is it Josh Schneiderman?

AC: Yes. I talked to him.

MG-S: When he told me what you were trying to do, I said it was a bad idea. Please do not use Frank. That's so unfair. It's using Frank to talk about a situation that is just between you and your father. It's very sad. You don't have any idea.

AC: I understand you feel that way.

MG-S: You don't understand, Ada! You don't understand at all! I can't work with someone who is not playing straight!

AC: I feel that I am playing straight. Would you like an apology from my father? Would that help with closure in some way?

MG-S: I would never demand an apology. Don't you get it? Frank would be so alien to this! Think about *that*! He would never even have bothered to call you as I have. It's very exploitative! I liked your book, but why would you talk about Auden that way?

AC: In what way? [I adore W. H. Auden. I told some stories about him in *St. Marks Is Dead* that are, if anything, hagiographic.]

MG-S: Why would you use those adjectives about him? [Later, I looked up the adjectives I used for Auden. They were: British, super-human, generous, gay, Christian.] Please spare Frank the journalist's approach. If you want to do the interviews, that's fine. You can't do the gossipy hearsay stuff. I've been through enough of that with other projects. I have liked and worked with so many people. I'm not

ADA CALHOUN

even going to tell you. I've known Kenneth, John, and everyone all these years.

AC: It was an honest question. I've only asked questions I genuinely wanted to know the answer to. I'm sorry it doesn't seem that way to you.

MG-S: I'm sure you really want to know.

AC: Okay. Thank you for calling. I understand that you don't support the project. May I ask if you will try to block it?

MG-S: [Laughs.] This is Harper all over again! That is exactly what they asked me! No. I don't intend to block anything by anyone. My message is simple. I personally don't like someone doing a biography who's not up to doing a biography. Unless people know the poetry well, they should not be writing about it. Other people have done fine things. Other people have done bad things. [Abstract expressionist painter Robert] Motherwell told me it was hard to have someone do a retrospective about your work. A biography is like a retrospective. It's daunting for the author.

AC: Perhaps you could tell me which writing about him you do like? You mentioned Marjorie Perloff. Is she one?

MG-S: See? This is how you are! I've known enough of your work to know this is how you think. You grab on to one thing I say, and you run with it. You think you know. I am glad you corresponded with me. I do not like the area. I don't know what you think you're going to straighten up. Write about your dad if you want to write about your dad. I don't get it. It's important for you to straighten this out. Maybe your dad should straighten his own life out. It has nothing to do with Frank. I had nothing to do with canceling his book. You have your new book coming out. Your father has his book. I haven't read it yet. You show me this proposal that you are going to send around to editors. I don't get it.

AC: Excuse me, but several times you have said something like "Your career is going well. You have a child. You have your life ahead of you." Forgive me, but it sounds menacing. Are you trying to say that if I go ahead with this project and write about Frank in some way, that these things will be in jeopardy? That I will be in danger somehow?

MG-S: This is ridiculous! So, it would be fine if I called your editor at Grove and asked if I could see your manuscript, without you knowing? Would you like that? Would you?

AC: Well, I don't think it's the same thing. If you were a journalist writing about me, I would expect you to try to read as much of my writing as you could. Of course, in this case I would also be happy to give you a copy myself. I want people to read my books.

MG-S: This is a ridiculous conversation! You really don't get it! They tried to do the project by contacting someone else! I'm more upset now about all this than when I called. Distress, distress! If you want to quote Frank's work, you may write for permission, but I do not get what you are trying to do. Distress, distress! Bye.

AC: Bye.

When we hung up, at 12:33 p.m., I was sweating through my St. Mark's Comics T-shirt. My face was red. I had a headache. How could I have failed so spectacularly to win her over? How could she have accused me of not playing straight, of not being up to the challenge? As a journalist, I'd successfully interviewed tempestuous stars and imprisoned felons. Why should writing something about a long-dead poet I loved prove so much more complicated than any of those assignments? And how was it possible that nothing I said helped my cause? Everything I said seemed to make it worse.

Here I'd been thinking that if only my father had played it differently, he would have finished his book. But I'd approached Maureen with diplomacy and care. She'd accused me of ignorance. She only blew off my father. She didn't even say why she'd disapproved of him until I started asking around forty years later. He was dismissed; I was castigated.

I emailed Josh and recapped the call, thinking he could help me understand what had just happened. He didn't write back for a while, which made me even more anxious. That evening, I took the subway deep into Brooklyn to do a bookstore reading. When I got home, I went straight to sleep.

At 5:33 a.m., I was wide awake, and there was one word in my head: *Vincent*. Vincent must have told Maureen what I said at our lunch. It explained everything: how she knew about the Dia reading and my conversation with Amei Wallach and my knowledge of the projects she's opposed.

Neal woke up to find me on the living room couch deep in conspiracy theories. I'd been betrayed! This was war and I had been compromised!

As he poured himself coffee, Neal asked, "When did this become all shadowy figures in trench coats with popped collars, flashlights darting through the night? Maureen's an old woman who manages a poetry estate."

I thought of what my father said about how everyone he talked to for the book seemed to be paranoid and watching their own reputation—everyone except Larry Rivers, who didn't care what anyone thought. He appreciated Larry Rivers because "at least he was actually *present*."

"It's strange and sad," Neal said, "how hard people hang on to things that don't really matter. This is not the Bay of Pigs. This is two successive generations of writers trying to say something of value about a wonderful, talented, funny young man who wrote lovely poetry and died in a freak accident. What a series of dying stars all collapsing in on each other: your dad's book, Maureen's machinations, your dad's poetry career, your attempts to win the scenario, your relationship with your dad, your relationship with Maureen. It's kind of amazing and beautiful—the ultimate unknowability of others."

I appreciated Neal's poetic take, but I did not find the situation remotely amazing or beautiful. I—teacher's pet of teacher's pets— had been dressed down by an authority figure, cast into the corner in a dunce cap. It was as though my 4:00 a.m. carousel of intrusive negative thoughts—*you're not good enough, your ideas are bad, you better watch out*—had come to life, taken on the aspect of an eighty-year-old woman in Connecticut. I felt misunderstood and embarrassed.

Worse, if I couldn't quote from O'Hara's work, I definitely couldn't do the book my father had wanted to do. Anything authorized or definitive was out. Anything I'd make out of this material would have to be some strange, subjective thing. If she'd just given me permission, I could have done a straightforward biography or an oral history, let everyone pontificate and gotten out of their way.

Then, as the days passed, my humiliation yielded to reflection. As I walked through the city from business meetings to school pickups to the grocery store, I kept trying to answer Maureen's questions, which boiled down to: *Why write about this?* Taking the question further: *Why write anything ever?*

I wonder if you'd get the same answer from me, from O'Hara, and from my father. I wonder if it's as simple as that we write to be known. To be seen. To be loved. To make rent. A part of me is writing this because I want people to know more about Frank O'Hara. But maybe, if I'm honest, what I also really want is for people to know about me, so I can feel like I left some mark on the world, however slight. As the novelist James Salter wrote, "There are stories one must tell, and years when one must tell them."

In 1983, my father said in an interview: "I think at the root of the critical impulse is some kind of adolescent outrage at growing up and discovering that the world is not nearly what you hoped or thought it might be. And that criticism is then a career of trying to move it over and make it more habitable for one's sensibility."

That sounds like what we do both as artists and as children: look at our parents, critique them like a work of art, figure out how we can make room for ourselves.

Aren't all stories ultimately, in one way or another, about the people writing them? On the last page of his memoir about his parents, writer Christopher Isherwood quotes a note his mother once wrote on a childhood project of his: "Perhaps, on closer examination, this book too may prove to be chiefly about Christopher."

I gather that there will always be people who see this desire to leave a trace as inherently selfish, mean, or dumb. When you write anything, you risk infuriating people, whether you're writing a pan of an artist or trying to tell the life story of someone you've never met. But if we never try to say anything about other people, who wins?

In "The Virtues of the Alterable," literary scholar Helen Vendler discusses an O'Hara poem about a night out dancing. She says, "Why is it worth recording? Because it happened. Why is what happened worth recording? Because what else is there to record? And why should we want to read it? Because what else is there to know except what has happened to people?"

I try to sort through the reasons Maureen gave for why she didn't support my project. She seemed mad that I interviewed people and that I wanted to go to the University of Connecticut to read material in the archive. But she's also mad that I don't know more about O'Hara. How would I learn more if I didn't do research? She accuses me of dealing in hearsay but says she won't tell me anything herself and seems mad that I've called some of the very few others who knew him and are still alive.

Maybe Maureen is right that I'm not smart enough to write about her brother. I've never even pretended to be as talented a writer as my father, who was also apparently not good enough for her.

I'm no poetry expert. I don't know much about classical music, either. I never learned how to play a musical instrument. I was too busy watching five hours of TV a day. But I've read a lot. And I do know some things. I know that in the late fifties, Frank O'Hara did a playful panel at the Club with Elaine de Kooning, Mike Goldberg, and Norman Bluhm. The panel's title? "Hearsay." O'Hara introduced the transcript by saying the panel's members had paid "careful attention to misattribution and misquotation in keeping with the spirit of the art world."

They comically misremembered and deliberately misidentified one source after another. Elaine quoted her mother: "Isn't it odd—thousands of years and the human race has come up with only five pieces of furniture." Bluhm quoted Mr. Wizard. Elaine quoted Emily Dickinson. O'Hara quoted Thoreau: "No matter how I try to think of Nature, my thoughts go constantly to plotting against the state." Goldberg quoted Elaine's brother Peter: "Why live simply when it's so easy to make life complicated."

I know grammar. I know what a zeugma is (*make me a millionaire and a dirty martini*).

I've lived pretty much my whole life in the city O'Hara loved. The movie theater where he watched *Rhapsody* once held 2,342 people. In 1969, it was torn down and the land was acquired by St. Vincent's Hospital, where I gave birth to my son in 2006.

I know that Frank O'Hara heard Stravinsky in the wind. I know he used listening to Robert Schumann as a pretext for inviting lovesick Larry Osgood up to his dorm room. I know he and Norman Bluhm listened to Tchaikovsky when they collaborated on poem-paintings. Do I need to know how to play these pieces of music, too, or what year they were composed and how to identify them after hearing sixteen bars? Or two bars? What amount of knowledge is enough?

Maureen asked me: *Why would you bring up something unattractive? Why would you write something that makes your father look bad?*

Because it's the truth. And if she had something she wanted to say, I would listen to her.

But apparently that call was what she wanted to say. And giving me that insight into the spirit that has guided her decades of estate management might be, in its own way, a gift.

In Henry James's *The Aspern Papers*, the narrator says, in response to a question about whether it's right to "rake up the past": "How can we get at it unless we dig a little? The present has such a rough way of treading it down."

Donald Allen said in his 1977 interview with my father that when he announced in 1957 that he was going to do a San Francisco issue of *Evergreen Review*, a well-meaning friend spent a whole dinner telling him it was a terrible idea. He left the dinner more determined to do the issue. That's how I feel too: a Frank O'Hara book is getting written by me now, by God. What book? Who knows? It seemed clear that Maureen would hate anything I did, whatever it was, and there was some liberation in that.

Reading back over my transcript of the call, which I do again and again, I'm sort of impressed with myself. I didn't cry. I didn't tell her she could have her way or promise to slink off without ever writing a word about her brother. I made it clear that if I couldn't have her blessing or her permission to quote from the work, I'd figure something else out.

And maybe what I'm figuring out is that the book I was meant to write was never a book about O'Hara—or even really about my father.

It was about me. My mother likes to tell the story that a therapist once advised her to "seek disapproval." This always seemed absurd to me. Approval was my drug of choice. But now, suddenly, I understand. Maureen's categorical disapproval has shown me the freedom that can come from defeat. The truth is, now I can say whatever I want. Quoting from O'Hara's poetry would be necessary for exegesis, and it was a requirement for any book about him before the Internet. But now anyone who wants to can google the poems while I talk about what O'Hara's friends said about him and about what it's like to live with him as my family's patron saint.

In a way, Maureen saved me from the hardship of crafting a conventional, academic biography she would sign off on. Now all other paths were open. O'Hara's friend Helen Frankenthaler said she had no plan when she went to paint: "There is no 'always.' No formula. There are no rules. Let the picture lead you where it must go." My father asked a version of this question each year when he judged a scarecrow contest at a local farm day: What does hay want to be? Finishing my father's book would be impossible; I would have to write my own.

Chapter 21

A month after Maureen's call, I get a phone message from my father:

Peter Schjeldahl—Voice Mail—6/2/19
One thing that's happened is that the *Village Voice* has reprinted my obituary of Frank O'Hara from 1966. I'm assured that it's going semiviral. And I just read it for the first time in fifty years. God, it's so grown-up. I must have had a great editor. Thinking of you and let's talk.

It's Saturday afternoon. While Oliver is at a weekend class, I'm working on a ghostwriting project at the Epiphany branch of the New York Public Library. I'm zipping through pages, fixing syntax, and dropping jokes into someone else's manuscript. Across from me at the library, an old man puts his earphones away in a Ziploc bag and tucks it into his pocket.

A few days ago, at a Mexican restaurant down the street from their apartment, my mother and I threw a book party for my father for his new book. The place was packed. My father's editor gave a flattering toast, Spencer gave a witty one, and my father graciously thanked everyone. There was applause. Just then, Steve Martin and his wife appeared behind him. Steve bowed as if the applause were for him, and everybody laughed.

My father looked like he was about to levitate from joy.

I ran into the artist and art writer Walter Robinson at the bar. He doesn't drink, so I ordered him a seltzer. He asked me about the sales for my dad's book.

"It's in the top thousand on Amazon," I said.

"Is that good?" he said.

"It's great," I said. "I don't think my last two books got that high."

"You need to step it up!" Walter said. "Or maybe you don't want to. In therapy, I learned that, at least for men, we don't always want to surpass our fathers. There's something sad about beating them."

Walter made me understand why as the weeks had passed since that call from Maureen, I'd begun to feel something like relief.

The Mexican restaurant grew louder and louder. The painter and Harvard student my father gave my room to that one summer, Matt, told me he'd read and loved my last book. I'd forgotten how much I liked him.

Vincent Katz was there. I told him that Maureen had called and yelled at me. He said not to take it to heart, that I should keep trying to win her over.

"Keep trying?" I said. "She told me I was no good, my dad was no good, and my idea was no good. I think that's game over."

He shrugged, as if none of that meant anything.

Poets, I thought. *They're such masochists.*

My father seemed aglow that night. He wasn't drinking, of course, but he seemed drunk on the attention. At the end of the party, I said goodbye to my parents and friends, then gathered up Oliver and his best friend, Stella, whom I'd given the job of manning the guest list at the door, and took them out for Chinese food. The three of us ate dumplings and laughed a lot, and as we walked through the city that night, I thought of what O'Hara said about the wind sounding like Stravinsky.

Chapter 22

"Frank O'Hara bounces off both of the ways people enjoy poetry—as an academic exercise and as lowbrow entertainment," my father said as I drove his black Subaru Forester—with him in the passenger seat. "He's scary like all truly great things are scary."

This car is scary, I thought, trying to leave plenty of space between me and the car in front of us. *And it's not truly great.*

When we're in the same car, I insist on driving because I hate my father's tendency to speed, dart in and out of lanes, and ride the brakes. But in this case, I was frightened even though I was driving, because the brakes were shot. He apparently hadn't noticed.

He'd just reread *The Tempest*. He was haunted by a particular scene, in which Prospero speaks to Ferdinand at the start of act 4:

> The solemn temples, the great globe itself,
> Yea, all which it inherit—shall dissolve
> And, like this insubstantial pageant faded,
> Leave not a rack behind. We are such stuff
> As dreams are made on, and our little life
> Is rounded with a sleep.

He said, "'Our little life is rounded in a sleep.' Isn't that wonderful? It's spatial. Life isn't short. It's little." He held his fingers together to show how small life was.

This seems like an ominous beginning to a week of medical testing, ordered because my father had suddenly lost a lot of weight. My mother, having left acting behind in the nineties, was spending more time upstate, where she had a store for ten years. She had just begun construction there on a Rip Van Winkle–themed miniature golf course, so I offered to take him to the battery: brain MRI, PET scan, biopsy.

I'd been down the medical-emergency road with him once before, a few years earlier. He'd fallen on the cobblestones of Chelsea while running for a bus and split his head open. Fellow New Yorkers had come to his aid and called an ambulance. In his haze, he gave my mother the wrong hospital name, and in her frenzy to get out the door she left behind her cell phone. I was the second call.

Behind a curtain, I'd found my father covered in blood and with a huge stitched-up bump on his head. There were bandage wrappers all over the bed. I was glad I'd arrived first so I could clean up and throw out all the bloody cotton before my mother got there.

As we faced this new round of tests, I was already in a kind of trance. Just a few weeks earlier, in July, my father-in-law, Lanny, a kind nurse who lived in Texas and won prizes for his intricate scale models, had suffered a catastrophic stroke and was in hospice care. He'd always been so nice to me. He bragged about my writing to his friends, had a photo of me on his wall and boxes of my writing in his closet, and often told me how glad he was that I'd married his son.

Neal flew to Texas as soon as we were called. A week later I followed with Blake and Oliver. Within days, we were told we should plan the funeral. We sat around the bed trying to think of what Lanny would have wanted. Neal suggested the song "The Old Rugged

Cross," and Lanny, who'd been unresponsive for days, raised his hand and pointed at Neal to tell us yes, that song. He died the next day.

Neal, his brother, our sister-in-law, and I cleaned out Lanny's apartment and storage units, settled the estate, threw the funeral, wrote thank-you notes, and drank margaritas. I took Oliver and Blake to JC Penney's for formal wear. One day in the church lobby, spacey from lack of sleep, I pointed to a painting of the apostles with a bunch of names underneath. Sure that my agnostic bohemian upbringing had deprived me of a good religious story, I said to my sister-in-law, Kari: "I know everybody here except one. Who's Wyatt?"

"The painter, Ada," Kari said, giggling and patting my shoulder. "There's no Apostle Wyatt." She later gave me a Saint Dolly Parton candle to honor my sketchy understanding of the sacred versus the profane.

Back in New York now for less than a month, I felt my mourning for Lanny cut short by my concern for the health of my father.

For days, I went with him to hospitals and doctors' offices on the Upper East Side—not a neighborhood I've ever particularly liked. When I was young, I barely ever went above Fourteenth Street except to go to the Met.

While my father was in recovery from his bronchoscopy, a procedure that sent a camera into his lungs and took tissue samples, I was told the surgery doctor would like to speak with me. I was shown alone into a room that held an orchid, a few chairs, and some flyers. One flyer read: "Turning to a chaplain for care and support."

Uh-oh, I thought. *This doesn't seem like the everything-is-fine room.*

A few minutes later, in walked the doctor, tall and striking, with graying hair and a strong face. He smiled at me. I felt a flicker of hope that he was about to whisk me off to one of the iconic Upper East Side bars I'd heard of but never been to. We could drink old-fashioneds in a booth at Bemelmans while we waited for my father to be discharged, first round on me. But after the initial smile, his face turned grave. He told me that the results would be ready in a few days but that I should know now: the lungs did not look healthy. He said what he saw was consistent with widespread cancer. He told me he was sorry.

The following days brought more paperwork and errands and waiting rooms. Hours spent keeping my father company and filling out forms and getting him new glasses. After one long day, I took him to a hip Brooklyn restaurant for a steak dinner because the doctor said he should try to put on weight. We were at an outdoor table, from which we could see my son's favorite playground, where over the years I'd spent hundreds upon hundreds of hours.

Life was precarious. Death felt close. And yet, here we were, eating good food together. We were talking easily, and it was nice. I looked at my father with affection. I thought of the O'Hara line about being out on a limb that happens to be God's arm. It's the most profound pun I ever heard.

Appearing sated and peaceful, my father looked back at me across the table. Smiling, he said, "I've been thinking, and I'm going to make Spencer my literary executor. I've already given him my old poetry. I'm also giving him money. He's a real starving artist."

I froze.

"Why do you want Spencer to be your executor?" I said, trying to hide how hurt I felt that after all we'd been through with Maureen, he would consider vesting that level of authority in someone he'd known for just a few years. I also felt shocked that he would consider taking those things away from my mother. She'd sacrificed so much of her own career and life to make his work possible. Because of her he'd never had to write a check, cook a meal, or clean a room.

"Doesn't Mom know your work at least as well?" I asked. "She's always been your first reader. I like to think I'd be competent, too. I've published a lot of books. I'm friends with editors at nearly every major publishing house. I have a powerful, smart literary agent. Why isn't any of that enough?"

I imagined that in my grief after my father died, I would be required to box everything up and give it to this young man I barely knew. I realized that all those months ago my therapist had been right: he was definitely capable of taking the O'Hara tapes away from me and giving them to someone else.

"Oh!" my father said. "Well! Spencer just knows my work so well! He's read *everything*. But I don't have to. It was just an idea."

At the next medical appointment, as we sat in the waiting room of yet another stupid office on the stupid Upper East Side, my father asked why, as he was chatting away, I was offering only one-word responses. I said it was because I was still mad about the literary-executor conversation. He said not to worry; he'd already talked to Spencer about it. He told Spencer I'd been upset by the idea so he couldn't give him control of the estate after all. Spencer was disappointed but ultimately understood.

I was quiet for a second and then I made a noise of shock that must have been loud because one of the other patients looked up in surprise.

"What now?" my father said, irritated.

"I can't believe you told Spencer you wanted to make him your executor but that I told you not to," I said, my voice shaking. "I can't believe you made me the villain, like I ruined an awesome party you guys were going to have."

"Spencer is my *best friend*!" he said. "I tell him *everything*!"

We sat in silence for a few minutes.

"You're trying to make Spencer and me hate each other," I said. "You want us to fight over you."

"That's *ridiculous!*" he said. He folded his arms and looked away.

I sat with my father while he had his blood drawn and an IV inserted. I sat in the waiting room for an hour while he went through the MRI. When he came out and we were walking to the subway, he said, "I thought about it while I was in the machine. Maybe you're right. Maybe I did a little bit want you and Spencer to fight over me."

When we returned to the East Village, I went out and bought cough medicine, groceries, and Veselka stuffed cabbage, then carried it all up to the top floor, the stairwell silent except for the shuffle of the plastic bags against my legs.

As we ate, I said, "One last thing about earlier. If you give Spencer your estate, you're not only taking something of value away from Mom, who won't have much income after you're gone, but it would also mean that I would have to go to Spencer to ask permission to quote from your writing. The Frank O'Hara tapes that you gave me? I would have to apply to Spencer for permission to use them. He would be within his rights to ask me to pay him for the privilege. Or, if he wanted to, he could do to me what Maureen did to us."

"It was just an idea," my father grumbled.

We ate our stuffed cabbage and kielbasa and then we started talking about other things. As I unwrapped the slice of chocolate cake, my father went to the bookcase. He found some old O'Hara books and told me to take them. Then he pulled a book of W. H. Auden's off the shelf and started to read one of his favorite poems: Auden's "In Memory of W. B. Yeats" (1940).

> He disappeared in the dead of winter.
> The brooks were frozen, the airports almost deserted,

And snow disfigured the public statues;
The mercury sank in the mouth of the dying day.
O, all the instruments agree
The day of his death was a dark cold day.

He read the whole poem, but for permission to share these six lines I had to sign two contracts and pay $285.37. So for the rest, please look up the poem for free on the Internet and imagine it being read in the top-floor kitchen of an East Village brownstone by a very thin man with a scraggly beard while his middle-aged daughter, looking tired, her hair in a ponytail, leans against the counter and listens.

Chapter 23

After my father's diagnosis, I feel haunted by the tapes. I've been pouring the voices of all these dead and dying people into my head and hoping I can do something with them. And the book project begins to feel more personal and more upsetting than I thought it would be. I try listening to the tapes again, hoping that I can get back to Frank O'Hara, which feels like safer ground. I turn to O'Hara's memorial service in the hope that the eulogies will help me make sense of his death and my father's, which might be imminent.

My father recorded the event from the audience at St. Mark's Church. At the front of the room were Jane Freilicher, Larry Rivers, and Kenneth Koch. Koch began.

Frank O'Hara's Memorial Service—East Village, New York City—1976
    Kenneth Koch: Frank died ten years ago. I have a few remarks, which
    will be very brief, and then I want friends of Frank's to take [over]
    from me. For all its cheer, and charm, and chumminess, for all its
    glamour and its gladness, I think we hear something else ten years
    later in Frank's poetry. *Now I am quietly waiting for / the catastrophe of*

my personality / to seem beautiful again, / and interesting, and modern.
There is a pervasive discontent in this work.

Koch read aloud from O'Hara's poetry and offered commentary. He said, "I think there's evidence that Frank O'Hara saw himself as *the* Byronic personality of our time"; and "Surely Frank would have recognized [his] death [on Fire Island] as the death of Hippolytus"; and "For all the laments and celebrations, we overhear the restless whimpers of a self desperately aware that time is being snatched out from underneath."

Jesus, I think. *Calm down.* I'd come to find nearly all these people irritating and self-important. Do they deserve to be resurrected? Maybe I should have let these tapes rot in the basement. I could have written a fun book, maybe *A Cultural History of Kittens.*

On the memorial service tape, a young poet named Michael Lally came up to talk about how reading Frank O'Hara made him believe poetry could be fun.

Larry Rivers made a snide remark. The crowd laughed. They couldn't get enough of him, even when he insisted that O'Hara's references to musicians like Billie Holiday were just shout-outs to his friends who cared about jazz (in other words, to Rivers).

Jane Freilicher, acting the diplomat, suggested that all the material in his life, all the names and facts he heard, acted as compost: "Everything is converted to soil eventually."

Koch kept providing anecdotes. In one, at the Cedar Tavern, Grove editor Barney Rosset supposedly said, "Frank, I'm really disappointed. I thought you'd come to more." And O'Hara said, in a nod to the poet Robert Graves: "What did you want me to do, go live on Majorca and take dope?"

Rivers kept cracking wise.

Larry Rivers: I figured out toward the end of his life that almost every-thing he did was about sex. Everything. Everything. And so, I think some of the collaborations were . . . I don't mean that they would get into bed necessarily, but there was some erotic *something* that was going. In fact, he collaborated with my children, my two male chil-dren. I think that even there, there was some kind of thing that had to do with that.

To be fair, Larry Rivers thought everything was about sex. Here he is writing about the Cedar Tavern in *New York* magazine in 1979: "What is a bar? Figured it out the other day—all it is, is about sex, really. And loneliness."

Why was I still listening to these people talk? I needed to focus attention on the present, where my father might be dying.

Chapter 24

Diagnosis day. A kind man with white hair who resembled a doctor in a children's book—the platonic ideal of Doctor—came into the room with a folder and sat down with us.

The scans, he said, showed many tumors, in both lungs and all through the body. The kind of cancer was "squamous cell lung cancer." The doctor said, "We can't cure this cancer, but we have treatments we can think about." He described the therapies. He said up until a couple of years ago the go-to would have been chemotherapy, which would have been exhausting and probably extended his life by just a few months, if at all. More recently, they'd begun to do immunotherapy instead of or in addition to chemo, with good effects.

The doctor said we only had to make one decision that day, "the first decision of a hundred more," and that was what treatment plan to start with. He said the options were chemotherapy, immunotherapy, both, or neither. We all sat there, stunned.

"What's your reaction when I mention chemotherapy?" the doctor asked.

"I'm a writer," my father said. "I'm still employed. I want to do whatever will help me keep writing as long as possible. I think chemo might make me too tired. Writing is the most important thing."

The room was quiet. Across from me, my mother's eyes were filled with tears. She looked scared.

"You're saying writing is what gets you out of bed in the morning," said the doctor, clarifying.

"The idea of not being able to write fills me with dread."

I couldn't believe what I was hearing.

"You aren't just a writer!" I said. "You're also a husband and a father and a grandfather and a friend."

Sounding exasperated, he said, "What am I supposed to do? Just sit around like a potted plant? I don't make any sense to myself if I'm not writing."

Another pause. My mother hadn't said a word.

"If I do nothing, how long have I got?" my father asked the doctor.

"Well, we speak in terms of median survival," the doctor said. "And with your kind of cancer and how far it's progressed, we say the median length of time after diagnosis would be six months. That means half live longer than that."

And, he did not say, that means half live shorter.

Six months. Once those words were spoken it felt like the weather in the room changed.

"I don't want to do chemo," my father said at last. He opted for immunotherapy. Probably no side effects. A 35 percent chance of improving his quality of life and possibly extending it. It would just mean an infusion every three weeks starting on Tuesday.

"I can't Tuesday," he said. "I have a deadline."

"That's okay," the doctor said. "If you're not done and can't make Tuesday, just call the office and move the appointment to Friday." I wondered what this kind, patient doctor thought of him, thought of us—this odd bohemian family, this workaholic patient.

The doctor broached the subject of quitting smoking.

"I don't want to quit," my father said. "I associate it with writing. When I try to quit, I don't understand what writers do anymore. I don't write."

I asked the doctor if changes like quitting smoking might prolong his life, which is what the bronchoscopy doctor had told me in that room with the chaplain pamphlets.

But this doctor didn't seem to want to push it. "This is a journey," he said. "It's hard to predict the various paths."

I wanted to grab him by the collar and say, "I know you have to say that, but stop being so philosophical! Make him quit smoking and then tell me exactly how long he'll live!" I wanted a death date I could circle in my calendar and plan around the same way when I was pregnant I wanted my due date to be the precise date I would give birth. (That didn't work either. Oliver was born eight days later, and not naturally at NYU but via emergency C-section and with every last monitor and drug at St. Vincent's.)

After the diagnosis appointment, I bought my parents food at a restaurant where in simpler times I'd eaten salads with a magazine editor. As we half-heartedly ate, I asked my father if he wanted to go on a trip to Europe or anything. He said, "Maybe a ballgame." I made a note to buy the best tickets I could afford.

A half hour later, we left the restaurant and found that it was raining. I was the only one who'd brought an umbrella. There were no cabs. My father said he wanted to walk to Chelsea to go look at art. I gave my father my umbrella and called a car for my mother to take her back to St. Marks. As I stood there alone in the rain in my least favorite neighborhood, I watched my father walk away. Before he rounded the corner, he lit a cigarette under the umbrella.

Aside from a few days or weeks or months here or there over the years, he's never been without a cigarette. For most of the past sixty years he's smoked three or four packs a day. He and George Montgomery talked about cigarettes in 1977.

George Montgomery—SoHo, New York City (791 Broadway)—3/28/77
Peter Schjeldahl: Can I steal . . . ?

George Montgomery: Sure.

PS: I want to get the full effect.

GM: Take a pack with you!

PS: No, I think I better stick to my filters. I might get a taste for them. Since I smoke three packs a day, I better.

GM: I smoke two packs a day. You can get them there on St. Marks Place, at the Gem Spa or something, at that corner place there.

PS: There's of course that great reference in "The Day Lady Died" about buying a carton of Picayunes at the Ziegfeld.

GM: I'd forgotten that Frank smoked them. We both learned to smoke them from someone else, a guy named Tommy Jackson, who'd been to Black Mountain, and they were the biggest-selling cigarette at Black Mountain.

PS: The literary cigarette.

GM: Oh yeah?

PS: Well, no, I'm saying . . .

GM: Oh. I don't know why. They're just a good cigarette, you know. I think Home Runs are made near North Carolina and they're made of the same tobacco as these. One either smoked one or the other.

PS: It is a very tasty cigarette.

GM: Isn't it? They don't cost any more than the others, so you don't have to worry about that.

PS: Well, I don't know. The lungs, the lungs . . .

Chapter 25

Maybe something about the word "treatment" put me in mind of "treats," because I couldn't stop buying my father the frozen yogurt he liked and books I thought might be helpful, like the book critic Anatole Broyard's cancer memoir *Intoxicated by My Illness*. I felt happy to serve him, especially now that he was writing thousands of words every day about his life. He didn't know if it would be a book or an article or something to put in a drawer, but it was the first writing he'd done for or about himself in decades and he was excited about it, so I was excited, too. I thought I should keep listening to the O'Hara tapes, but I figured that could wait. What was important now was helping my father do what he needed to do before he died—and to help my mother cope.

I acted as an as-needed caretaker for my parents' apartment because they were in the Catskills. When I went by to let a plumber in to fix the toilet, I found the place filthy. Before he joined my mother upstate, my father had been alone in the city for weeks, and it showed. The office was full of ashes and dust. The sheets were stained by the chocolate he ate in bed. The blankets, stuffing escaping, were covered in grime. My father never cleaned the house. He rarely even washed his hands—an affectation buoyed by something he once read about how allergies are caused by being overly hygienic.

I went to change the sheets but couldn't find any fresh ones. I took a bag full of laundry to the laundromat, and I bought new sheets and blankets at the Astor Place K-Mart. While at the store, I also bought a humidifier and cough drops. For the first decade of my career, I was always in debt. Neal and I fought about money all the time. These days, ghostwriting and the sale of my book about Generation X had made me more financially secure than I'd ever been. For the first time I could spend a couple hundred dollars on my parents' comfort without worrying.

When I returned from the store, I vacuumed—there were wrappers and loose pills scattered around the bed—and mopped, then put the new bedding on the bed and set the cough drops in a bowl next to the humidifier. *If he's going to die here*, I thought, *it will be as comfortable as I can make it.*

For a couple of weeks after his diagnosis, my father floated around in a pink cloud. He was gentle and kind and paid attention to people. My mother said he hadn't been like this since before they were married. She seemed happy to have him this way again.

So much of O'Hara's poetry, I realize now, exists in this sort of brink-of-death pink cloud. In his eulogy for O'Hara, the composer Morton Feldman wrote: "Who but the dead know what it is to be alive? Death seems the only metaphor distant enough to truly measure our existence. Frank understood this. That is why these poems, so colloquial, so conversational, nevertheless seem to be reaching us from some other, infinitely distant place. Bad artists throughout history have always tried to make their art like life. Only the artist who is close to his own life gives us an art that is like death."

During the pink-cloud time, I took my father to a Mets game along with my mother, Neal, Oliver, and family friends Kent and Deborah. Kent, a great doctor, had steered my father to the best medical care. For that, I would have loved him even if he weren't the funniest and nicest of my parents' friends. As we were waiting for the rest of our party by the worn home run apple in the Citi Field parking lot, my father said, "Self-knowledge is maybe better never than too late."

"That's not true!" I said.

"I was kidding. I've been thinking of what you said about the effect I have on people. It's when I feel most relaxed that I say these things that make them mad. I get too comfortable. And then I try to say something witty, but they come out clever and that makes people run away and then I wonder why I'm all alone."

"Huh," I said. "That makes sense. It is true. Clever pushes people away; witty draws people close. Frank O'Hara was witty. He made other people feel at ease."

At the game, Oliver caught a T-shirt from the T-shirt cannon, which my father took to be a sign of divine approbation. Then Robinson Canó tried to throw Oliver a ball, looked right in his eyes, but an adult snagged it out of the air instead and I wondered if that was a form of divine judgment, too.

Pete Alonso hit a historic home run. I bought my father a big ice-cream sundae in a baseball hat. After he ate it and the rest of Oliver's sundae, he began feeling dizzy. His hands turned blue. Kent suggested he put his head between his knees for a little while. The guys in front of us turned around and said they, too, were doctors, if we needed anything. The decision was made to leave in the seventh inning. My father didn't want to set a bad example for Oliver by leaving early—we were never allowed to go early when I was a kid—but he was tired. And so I drove him back to St. Marks Place, and my mother helped him up the stairs and into the bed with the crisp new sheets.

Chapter 26

The weather turned cool. I had drinks with the publicity team at Grove, my new publisher. They asked what I wanted to do for a tour. They knew my father was sick and delicately inquired as to whether I felt okay about traveling. I said I wanted to do my job, to promote the book for all our sakes. I could come back to the city once a week or so.

I must have sounded heartless, like I cared more about being a writer than about anything else. But the truth was, my father didn't seem much to need me around anyway. He talked to Spencer every day. The only times I saw him were when I called and made a plan to go over.

"Of course your father would rather hang out with Spencer than with you," Neal told me. "You don't fit in with their friends like he does. You don't care about the art world. You hold yourself apart, skeptical. You see through your father. You and your mother give him a hard time. Spencer is just fun and full of praise. Who would you rather have lunch with? Someone who was always feeling hurt by you or someone who told you all the time that you were great?"

More than jealousy for his time, I increasingly felt envy for his professional life. If you lock yourself away from your family your work gets to go deeper. I've been distracted for most of my life, certainly for the thirteen years since I became a mother. I've written in libraries, in coffee shops, and once on the couch in the middle of an active Nerf gun battle between my son and several neighbor children. It's possible that the best work I've done was several years ago at the artists' colony MacDowell, where for two weeks I did exactly what my father has always done—shut everyone else out.

When I told my parents I was going to do that, my father rolled his eyes. He thought residencies were lame. He said he wouldn't be caught dead at a writers' colony. My mother snapped at him: "Your whole life is a writer's colony."

It was true. He'd lived his whole life for writing. I always just did it when I could, after I made sure my son was taken care of. Would I be a better writer if I had an office at home with a door that locked? If I hadn't helped Oliver with his homework? If we didn't eat dinner together as a family every night?

From the moment Oliver started eating solid food, he loved cucumbers. Whenever we ate out, I would pick the cucumber slices out of my salad and give them to him. I cut up cucumbers when he wanted a snack and served them, lightly covered in salt, in a little bowl. In the decade since, I have not eaten very many cucumbers myself. If there are cucumbers, they go on his plate, not mine. Cucumbers are his thing. I don't even ask myself whether I like them. Art was my father's thing. He piled it high on his plate. It didn't occur to me to get any for myself. If he offered to share it, I refused. *No*, I thought. *That's yours.*

And it's not martyrdom. My favorite thing to do is to take trips with Oliver and Neal. We've gone out West, where we drove through deserts and walked through canyons; to England, where Oliver marveled over every pasty and cup of tea; and to Cuba, where we explored Communist museums and cave paintings. Those are the best memories of my life. Still, I sometimes wonder if I would be as celebrated a writer as my father if I'd stayed single, childless, cloistered. To be a great writer or artist, how ruthless do you need to be? How single-minded? Do you have to be the kind of ruthless where in front of your wife of forty-seven years you tell your doctor that you only care about writing?

If I'd had more children, as I'd always thought I would, would I have written any books at all? I longed for another baby when Oliver was a few years old. Since then, I've published a book every two years or so, at the same rate that in another era I'd have given birth. I'm content with my compromises except when I see a toddler girl with barrettes in her hair. Then I think, *I should have five of those, lined up in a row on my Christmas card. If it meant I wrote half as many books—or no books—so what?*

Perhaps my role as a writer who is not the best writer in my family is the cost of paying attention to my family. Or maybe I should have picked one kind of writing and stuck with it rather than switching every few years. My father wrote poetry for a decade and art criticism for forty years. In the past twenty years I've done national news reporting, New York City history, memoir, and generational lament. Maybe my real problem is that I'm too easily distracted, every year on to the next shiny thing. If only I were more serious. If only I'd gone to an Ivy League school and gotten a more classical education like those terrible Harvard kids. The roulette wheel of self-recrimination always stops in the same place: if only I were a different person, I could be really great.

"Should I have closed a door on my family?" I asked my shrink. "Would I be a better writer, as good as my dad?"

"Your father had a thirty-four-year head start," she said. "Oliver will be out of the house in less than five years. Then you can close a door and work all day every day for forty years if you want. Personally, I'd rather read something by someone who had a full life before locking out the world." I find what she says—you can have everything, maybe just not all at once—comforting, though I fear she's humoring me.

Over at my parents' place after I'd brought them soup and more frozen yogurt, my father, still in his pink cloud, told me he wanted to hear anything I had to say to him.

I looked across the table and realized he meant it. I commended him for asking. I was surprised and impressed that he seemed so open. It felt new. I said, "I think I've said it all before but maybe this will be a little clearer. You've said you didn't think I liked Spencer. I've only met him a couple of times, but I liked him. He seems smart and helpful, and he makes you happy. If I bristle when you talk about him, it might be because of what he symbolizes. He's the latest in a very long list of Things or People You Are Way More Interested in Than Me: alcohol, AA, art, fireworks, writing, and those Harvard students who talked to me like I was their maid.

"You hated your parents for never seeing you. I could have hated you for never seeing me, but I don't. I love you. And in the end, I'm grateful. If you had paid real attention to me at any point, would I have worked so hard and done so much trying to be worthy of attention? Maybe not. Your disinterest has been at once the saddest part of my childhood and the greatest gift of my life.

"When you heard you were dying, the first words out of your mouth were 'I'm a writer.' You didn't look at Mom, but if you'd seen her eyes! I think you see what Spencer does for you, but I don't think you see what she does. She's given you a fifty-year writing residency. Since your diagnosis, she and I have both made it possible for you to keep doing your favorite things: smoking, writing, hanging out with Spencer. I just want you to consider that other people in your situation might have other priorities right now."

He thanked me for my honesty, and he seemed to take it in.

When I got home, I told Neal what I'd said, and I asked him why I felt so crummy even though I was glad I'd said it. He said, "Maybe part of you hoped that when you told him he'd never found you interesting, he'd say you were wrong."

Chapter 27

On the road for my book's prepublication tour, I traveled to trade shows in Denver, Portland, and Cleveland. At ballrooms in each city, I attended parties and sipped wine and carried around tote bags full of other writers' advanced reader copies.

I took the train to Massachusetts to appear onstage at the Boston Book Festival in front of hundreds of people at a historic church. The night before the event I went to put on a new dress and old boots to head to the welcome party at the huge library near my hotel. Only it turned out I had brought two different boots: the left of a pair with three-inch heels and the right of a pair with four-inch heels.

I looked at my phone map and found that there was a department store on the way to the event, so I put my sneakers on with my dress and stopped off there. As I was trying on pairs of discounted black boots, my phone vibrated. It was an email from the Grove publicist. My Gen X book had just gotten a rave from *Publishers Weekly*. They called it a "bracing, empowering study . . . humorous and pragmatic." My editors at Grove instructed me to have extra drinks that night. I promised I wouldn't let them down.

At the party, I stood in the library's lobby and gossiped with friends I hadn't seen in a while. I ate single-serve noodles out of a box. A bunch of writers swept me into a procession to a nearby bar, where we laughed and drank and snacked for hours. Back at my hotel later that night, on the plush bed, I fell asleep happy.

The next morning, I woke up at 7:00 a.m., several hours before I was supposed to take the festival stage. I planned to go back to sleep. But first I checked my phone. I saw a voice mail from a Waltham, Massachusetts, number, left at 2:22 a.m. Probably spam. Just to be sure, I pushed Play.

Brooke Alderson—Voice Mail—10/19/19

Hi, Ada. It's Mom, calling you probably close to two o'clock in the morning and um, we're out on the street because we had a fire in the apartment. And we're trying to figure out what we're going to do. This phone is an EMS worker's so it's not— Unless you get this within the next ten minutes or so I think it's not going to be valid. I will try and call later, or I'll let you know where we are at some point. Okay, talk to you in a little while. Bye.

My mother sounded calm. But she didn't give me very much information. I called their apartment number, and it was out of service. I called her cell and my father's—straight to voice mail. I checked the *New York Times*, *New York Post*, and NY1 and found no mention of an East Village fire, so I thought it couldn't have been serious. Then I looked on the neighborhood app Citizen and saw there had been a fire on St. Marks Place the night before. Some guy on the next block who kept burping shot a video from his window of the flames between First and Second Avenues. It looked like my parents' part of the block, and it looked bad. Fire trucks lined the street.

I called the Ninth Precinct. The dispatcher said there'd been a shift change, but he asked around to find someone who was on duty the night before. After a while, the man on the phone returned and told me: "There were no displacements." I asked if that meant they got back into the apartment and the cop on duty said yes, that must be the case or there would be information about where they were taken. I guessed the options were a hospital, shelter, or morgue. I was relieved. It must not have been that big a fire. Still, I was worried that I couldn't get either of my parents on the phone and that the last I'd heard from them was five hours earlier, as they'd stood on the street watching their home burn.

I called Neal and woke him up. I asked him to go to St. Marks Place to see if they were back in the apartment. I made hotel-room coffee and ate a granola bar and took a shower and felt helpless. Neal called about an hour later and put my mother on. He'd found her at the building, but no one had stayed there the night before. No one would be staying in that building for a long time. Every surface was covered with rubble and water and soot. On the phone, I learned that my parents had slept a few hours at their next-door neighbor George's place, at 55 St. Marks. To soothe their nerves, George had given my mother a glass of scotch and bought cigarettes for my father from the corner store, Gem Spa.

My mother told me what they knew: at around 1:30 a.m. my father had woken up in dense smoke. It was a miracle he woke up at all given how many drugs he was on because of the cancer—Ambien, Xanax, codeine.

On his way out of the bedroom, he opened the door to his office and flames shot out. He went to the front room, woke up my mother, who was sleeping in my old room because he coughed so much at night. They fled down the four flights of stairs in their bare feet. As they stood outside watching the building burn, neighbors came running outside to bring them shoes and coats. A representative of the Red Cross appeared and gave them blankets and a gift card for $250, which they promptly lost. One cat, Theo, was carried out unconscious in his cat bed and revived by a fireman with an oxygen mask. The other cat, Bertie, could not be found.

My father was afraid he'd started the fire with a cigarette and went up to a fireman to tell him that. The fireman said that given what they'd seen so far he was almost certainly not the culprit. Later they would learn that an electrical fire had started inside the bathroom ceiling of their neighbor's apartment, which was under construction. Given how charred the joist was, the fire had probably been burning for hours in the floor below his office, directly under his desk.

Marooned in Boston, I wondered if I should get the next train. But my publisher had already paid for my hotel room and train ticket. I figured I should go onstage at the appointed time and then take off right after, skipping the remaining parties. I changed the time of my ticket and packed.

When I arrived at the festival holding area carrying my bag, I told the moderator what had happened.

"Oh no!" she said. "Did you lose all your family photos?"

That hadn't occurred to me.

"I guess so," I said.

During the event, the moderator mentioned that I epitomized the "sandwich generation" phenomenon and that in fact there'd been a fire the night before in my parents' home and my father was already dying from cancer. I said that was true and then I changed the subject.

Chapter 28

My train pulled into Penn Station after dinner, and I talked to my mother on the phone as I walked home to Neal and Oliver. My parents were staying one more night with their neighbor George. Then we'd move them to a hotel for a few days. I wished we had a big place with a guest room rather than a tiny Brooklyn apartment without the floor space even for a full-size air mattress.

The next morning, I arrived at George's apartment, bearing new glasses for my father that I'd rush ordered. My parents both seemed shell-shocked, and yet my mother was somehow in full makeup she'd been able to salvage from the destroyed apartment.

"Of course you have mascara on!" I said, and she smiled.

I got my father a new computer from the Union Square Best Buy and new Converse sneakers, and I got them each bags of new-old clothes I thought they'd like from Buffalo Exchange.

"We'd like you to do the thinking for us," my father told me.

Each evening for the coming weeks, I arrived at my parents' temporary quarters—a hotel, then another friend's empty apartment, then an Airbnb—bearing bags full of things they needed: socks, underwear, vodka, a cashier's check for the furnished East Village sublet I'd helped them find, the insurance inventory I'd assembled (three times greater than the maximum they could get from their policy), takeout.

Neal and I kept their cat Theo at our place in Brooklyn. Smelling like smoke, he slept all night by our heads, purring, and spent the days staring in reverential awe at Oliver's pet turtle. I went full *Saving Private Ryan* on the other cat, Bertie. When people asked what they could do to help, I told them to look for Bertie. I filed his picture with multiple databases so if he wound up at a shelter he wouldn't be destroyed. I posted flyers around the neighborhood.

With my mother, I spent hours each day going through rubble at the St. Marks apartment. All the windows and skylights were bashed out. Pieces of roof beams lay on the floor like piles of kindling. My father's office was ash. Gone were all his papers and the dictionary I used to look words up in when I was a little girl. A hole in the floor gaped, revealing the apartment below. Bookshelves from which my father had pulled the Nakian catalog and the Donald Allen boxes were charred, the remaining books looking like slices of bread long forgotten in a toaster.

I wondered if the O'Hara appointment books had been in some neglected drawer. I should have violated my father's privacy and done a proper search, I thought, when I'd had the chance. I'd worried about whether I'd have to share my father's papers and books with Spencer. Now that worry was gone. There were no more treasures to covet.

With glass and cement crunching underfoot, sweating behind the mask I wore to keep out the fumes, I gathered all the surviving art, some now sporting fireman bootprints, into the front room. I called handlers who could take it for restoration. I collected family photos—many waterlogged but salvageable—and took them home. I brushed grit from Polaroids of my elementary-school birthday parties, cabinet cards of anonymous ancestors, and little black-and-white prints of my parents in the 1960s. I spread them out around my apartment on towels.

No matter how much Febreze and apple cider vinegar and Lysol and dish soap I threw at everything, whatever I took out of that apartment kept the acrid smell. A housefire odor is the opposite of a campfire smell. Rather than burning sticks and sizzling food, this scent was melting plastic, sparking wires, shower curtains fusing to curtain rods.

My parents' whole building was uninhabitable—the top because the fire had burned it and the bottom because the fire hoses had flooded it. That week we learned a phrase: "Fire goes up; water goes down." Smoke is greasy. That's why it's so hard to get rid of the smell. All the walls throughout the building would have to be opened and treated for mold.

Out in the world, I kept misspeaking, as if half my brain was doing something else and I was only half there. I fell down three times in three weeks—missing a step, misjudging the curb, stumbling on the subway platform. Time made no sense. I lost track.

My therapist said it was because I hadn't had time to metabolize the present, so the past and future were getting a little abstract. "It's like a snow globe," she said. "When it keeps getting shaken up, the snow never settles down enough for you to see."

One afternoon, my parents and I met up at the apartment to do yet another pass through it, looking for things to save. In the living room, my father fixated on a Duke Snyder–signed baseball in a little plexiglass display box. He picked it up, carried it around for a while, then set it down while he looked through another room. As he was looking in that room, he called to me to help him find the ball because he'd forgotten where he'd put it. I found it in the hallway and gave it back to him. Then I found a little model of a Spitfire plane made out of the remains of an actual Spitfire and asked him if he wanted to take that. He did. I asked if he also wanted a little antique futuristic toy car I'd found. He did. He seemed happy holding the ball and car and plane.

I felt a surge of maternal love for him, the same kind I'd felt years before watching Oliver fall asleep in his car seat or shriek on the playground swings.

Turning back to the apartment, though, I felt despair. A few weeks earlier I'd been mopping these floors and putting pillows in fresh new pillowcases. And to what end? Would anyone ever be able to live here again? What a waste that I'd bought new blankets.

Then I thought of a line attributed to Martin Luther: "If I knew the world was to end tomorrow, I would still plant an apple tree today."

There's a line like that in *Middlemarch*, too: "That by desiring what is perfectly good, even when we don't quite know what it is and cannot do what we would, we are part of divine power against evil—widening the skirts of light and making the struggle with darkness narrower."

My desire for the good took me once again to K-Mart. While I was pushing my cart, loaded with more necessities for my parents—Ensure, A&W root beer, yet another humidifier—my phone rang. It was one of my parents' oldest friends, Katie Schneeman, who lived down the street at 29 St. Marks Place.

"Well, it's good that the fire wasn't so bad," she said.

She was going deaf, so I had to speak loudly to make myself heard.

"It was bad, Katie!" I yelled into the phone, probably startling fellow shoppers. "The whole back half of the apartment was destroyed. There's a ton of smoke and water damage and they can't live there for a long time. The whole building is empty now and will be until they can fix the roof and the electrical system and the hallways."

"What?" she said.

"EVERYTHING BURNED!" I yelled into the phone. My voice echoed down the cat food aisle.

★ ★ ★

While nothing was left of my father's office, some things of his did survive: the chapbooks he pulled off the bookshelf that night he read me the Auden poem about Yeats, the Donald Allen boxes he gave me that time after dinner, the poetry he gave Spencer, the O'Hara tapes.

But it had gotten so that I couldn't bear to listen to the tapes anymore. I kept thinking about how all those people were dead and about how soon my father might be, too. I worried about the cancer and about how reckless he was with his body. He was still smoking. Every time I checked on his meds, I found him taking too much. When I brought him the new humidifier, I saw that he'd taken fifteen doses of codeine cough syrup in the time he was supposed to have taken two.

Then, a miracle: Bertie, the missing cat, was found in a neighbor's closet. He'd been living on toilet water and mice, the New York City wonder diet. A stone had been rolled away and a crypt found empty. There was rejoicing in the East Village.

Of Frank O'Hara, critic Geoffrey O'Brien once wrote: "He welcomes whatever is incomplete, interrupted, unplanned: anything that contradicts the orderly completeness of death." Here now was this cat back from the dead: this otherwise unremarkable animal eating Fancy Feast, sleeping at the foot of the bed, using the litter box—every moment a thumb in the eye of Death.

Chapter 29

At a creaky old Catholic college building in Washington, DC, I was about to appear on a panel about essay writing for a book festival when my phone rang. It was my father. I was early—the first one in the room. On the white tablecloth sat my nameplate, my lukewarm coffee, and a few pieces of melon on a sagging paper plate. Outside the window were brochure-worthy trees turning orange and red and yellow. I answered.

"I just heard back about the scan," he said. "The immunotherapy worked. I'm part of the thirty-five percent!"

I went with my parents to my father's next Memorial Sloan Kettering appointment.

We were told the tumors had shrunk by more than half. He was not cured, but he probably had extra time now and would likely cough less. The doctor asked how he was feeling.

"Tired. Depressed," he said. "All I want to do is write and I can't concentrate." The pink cloud had dissipated.

"You could retire," the doctor said, smiling but serious. "People do retire, you know."

My father shook his head.

"How about therapy?" the doctor asked.

"I suppose it might feel good to rattle away to someone for fifty minutes without feeling like I had to apologize for it," he said. But it was clear he wouldn't pursue that course of action.

He weighed 128 pounds. His eyes looked huge behind his glasses. He'd grown a gray beard. Add a ruff collar and he could be in an old masters painting. When he pulled up his shirt to show the doctor his chest, I saw his pale, thin body. He joked that he was playing host to a gang war between the immunotherapy and the cancer, with both living off the land.

My father asked if he could have something for his low energy. The doctor said they could look into steroids at some point.

"Oh!" my father replied, brightening. "I used to love speed. That could be great if—"

"I loved speed, too!" my mother chimed in.

The two began chattering about how in the 1960s they took speed all the time, how they got so much done.

"Okay, that's enough," I said.

"It made you crazy, though," my father said to my mother, ignoring me. "When we started dating, I made her throw it out," he told the doctor.

"And you thought I did!" my mother said, laughing girlishly.

"Will you both please stop talking about how much you love speed!" I said. "Speed is not even on the table here. The doctor is talking about your maybe trying *steroids* at some point. Steroids are not amphetamines."

"Oh," my father said, looking disappointed.

My mother, as she rummaged in her purse for a stick of gum, whispered, "I did love speed, though."

★　★　★

Afterward, in the waiting room, between the doctor meeting and the immunotherapy infusion, we got an email from my father's sister Ann. My grandmother was going downhill. She had developed an infection and was having hallucinations.

We discussed Grammy and who should go up to visit her when. Then I mentioned that Oliver had gone on a class trip to Madison Square Garden that day, along with thousands of other public-school students, to see a stage production of *To Kill a Mockingbird*. I told them that the mayor had come onstage to introduce the event and a ton of kids had booed him. New York!

"Does he like *To Kill a Mockingbird*?" my father asked.

"Yes," I said. "Remember, he tried to talk to you about it once and you told him: 'It's no *Huckleberry Finn*'?"

Across the waiting-room chair between us, my father held out his hand for me to hit, like he was a naughty student and I a schoolmarm. His hand looked pale and frail, with long yellow nails. I gently tapped it.

I said that I didn't want to keep giving him a hard time but that I wondered if maybe he wouldn't be so depressed about writing if he placed value on other things in his life, too. Maybe he'd want to hang out with his grandson, for instance, or take a trip with my mother. "You keep saying you're *just a writer*," I said. "But it's not true. Maybe writing is the thing you're most comfortable doing. Maybe you feel loved best for how well you write. But you have other things."

"It's not about getting love," he said. "I'm just driven."

"*I'm* driven," I snapped. "I've written eighteen books in the past ten years. I would still never look at my child and say writing was the only thing I cared about."

Chapter 30

"Do you want to keep any of these pans?" I asked my mother as we worked our way through another pile of rubble on St. Marks Place. We stared at the pots she'd used to host all those dinner parties. All were blackened; many were broken. They littered the countertops, full of moldy water and soot. In the back of the apartment, water poured through the ceiling. Nothing stood any longer between the clouds and the apartment floor.

My mother and I did debris removal for hours, stuck in a cloud of foul air because the windows were all still boarded up with plywood. We made piles of things to throw away. We cleaned out the closets, with their boxes of ornaments, and the desk with my old Garbage Pail Kids in the drawer, and the bookshelf with my great-uncle's P. G. Wodehouse books. When we left, our clothes were blackened and permeated with the smell of something gone very wrong. While we were scavenging, I found a clock in the rubble, mostly melted, stopped at 1:30—right around the time of night my parents were running for their lives down the stairs.

My throat felt raw. The cold and the dirty air made it worse. The demolition guy showed up in his emergency-services jacket and baseball cap and told us that before the apartment could be rebuilt it would be "taken to the walls," turned into a big empty box. My mother and I looked at each other and looked around and didn't have anything to say. *Sure, tear down all the walls*, I thought. *At this point, why not?*

After we finished working, we got some food and brought takeout to my father.

"I've been rereading Simone Weil's *Gravity and Grace*," he said. "Do you know her?"

"I ordered you that book," I said. "Didn't you read the note that came with it?"

"Oh!" he said. "I was sort of wondering why it showed up."

One night after seeing a play, my friend Jason and I walked through Times Square to catch the subway to our respective parts of Brooklyn. I told him the original Frank O'Hara book idea was dead and I was trying to figure out what to do with the material.

"Would you *go there* with the book?" he asked me. "Talk about the problems you've had with your father?"

"Probably not," I said. "It's not like I was abused. Besides, it's hard to write a memoir while you're living it. It's like eating a cake while it's baking. Maybe after he dies, I'll be able to make some sense of it."

"Come on!" Jason said. "Take no prisoners!"

I thought of the John Ashbery line:

> Take no prisoners.
> Fine. I don't want any prisoners.

I tell Jason I don't know what the book is about; the way this year is going, I feel like I don't know *anything*.

Chapter 31

For as long as I can remember, my father's contribution to the New Yorker Festival has been to lead ticket holders through a tour of the Frick Collection—the Upper East Side mansion containing industrialist Henry Clay Frick's collection of old masters. This year, Neal, Oliver, my mother, and I went along. The tickets were supposed to be $250, but he got us comped; he said they couldn't say no to the request because he had cancer. Oliver followed along, standing in the front row, a smiling, eager student. I mostly stayed in the back, feeling guilt at not having paid and sulking because my father denied my request to record his talk.

Every pill in every rug and every inch of wallpaper in the Frick is just so. The guards are merciless. In the biggest room, several people were taking photos of my dad with their phones, including Alexis, who worked there, so I took out my phone to take a quick photo, too. As I raised it, a guard flew to my side and hissed into my ear, "You can't take photos here!"

I looked around at the others taking photos, then at the angry face of the guard, so close to mine that I could see her freckles, and I felt confused. People in front of me turned around to see who had just gotten into trouble. They no doubt felt the same schadenfreude I'd experienced minutes earlier when a white-haired woman leaned against a table and a guard acted as though she'd taken out a can of spray paint.

"No, she can," Alexis said to the guard. "It's okay," Alexis said to me, "I just forgot to tell her that you could. Go ahead." I heard Alexis whisper something to the guard. Probably something like "That's her dad. He's dying."

I no longer wanted to take a picture, but Alexis was looking at me expectantly. I raised my phone, took a quick photo—blurry, I'd see later, useless—and put my phone away. We moved into the Fragonard room. This was where Frick's lady guests retired after dinner to play cards surrounded by cupids.

I felt myself start to cry. I hated getting in trouble. I pushed down the tears. The last thing I wanted to do was call attention to myself again—or to distract my father. If Alexis, or my mother, or Neal, or Oliver saw me, they would ask what was wrong and then I would cry more. I thought about excusing myself to the restroom to splash water on my face, but then I remembered that one of the rules was that a guard had to escort us if we broke off from the group for any reason.

As my father talked about the Fragonards, I felt my face grow hot. I was glad I had on glasses, thinking they might hide my face a bit. I wondered if I should switch them out for my sunglasses or if that would attract more attention. I tried to distract myself by staring hard at the paintings. My father pointed to the cupid stabbing a dove and said he'd asked many experts about the image's meaning, but there was no consensus. Something about jealousy, probably.

By the time we'd moved on to Rembrandt's 1658 self-portrait, I was calmer. My father said that the painting made him emotional. In it, Rembrandt was fifty-two. His affair with a maid had been a scandal. A child had died. In his eyes, my father said, "You can see that he knows he is the best painter in the world, but he's not sure it amounts to a hill of beans."

We were directed to the next Rembrandt painting, *The Polish Rider*. A young man sits on the back of a horse in motion. "He's a killer who hasn't killed yet," my father said. "His eyes are hard, but his mouth is soft. By the end of this day, his mouth will be hard like his eyes." He added that this was a favorite picture of Frank O'Hara's, who spoke of his admiration for the young rider's body.

At the Q&A upstairs, strangers asked my father questions. One was who his mentors were. He said Baudelaire, Apollinaire, Gertrude Stein, "and absolutely Frank O'Hara, in writing and on art."

On the way out the door, my father asked if Oliver had learned something. Oliver hugged him and said that yes, he especially liked the part about the Polish soldier's eyes.

On the subway ride home, Oliver told me that he liked that kind of painting more than modern art, which he pretty much never liked.

"That makes me sad!" I said, even though when I was his age, I felt the same way. "It's so brave of artists to do what they do, to say, *Look, I made this and it's important*. They're trying to tell us something that's too complicated for a conversation. Same with poets. If they could say it plainer, I think they would. But there's something deeper that they have to say and maybe they need to say it with an all-white canvas or in little lines that make you feel something different. Or in a song."

Oliver said he liked Seurat because he respects the skill that takes, but he doesn't understand why Pollock is revered when anyone could do that.

"Why is it bad if you think you could do that, too?" I said. "Why isn't it liberating, like punk rock? And if you could so easily make something moving out of paint, why don't you?"

I heard myself using the same overearnest tone Doris Walker used when speaking to her daughter, Susie, at the end of *Miracle on 34th Street*: "You must believe in Mr. Kringle and keep right on doing it!"

Going online to find a book to give Oliver about abstract art, I found a pamphlet: *What's with Modern Art?* by Frank O'Hara. According to the copyright page, Maureen gave permission to Mike and Dale's Press in Austin, Texas, in 1999 to print fifteen hundred copies of the chapbook. It's a collection of O'Hara's short reviews and a reprint of a one-page item in *Ingenue* magazine from December 1964 called "Teens Quiz a Critic: 'What's with Modern Art?'"

In the article, O'Hara, in his role as assistant curator at MoMA, answers teenagers' questions. The first is about what it means when an artist splashes paint on a canvas. He replies that if a person devotes effort to something like that it means that he's serious and he's trying to communicate something. He also says that "as at the beach, a splash can be a very beautiful thing."

Chapter 32

As the sun set on Thanksgiving afternoon at my parents' place upstate, I leaned my shoulders against the mantle of the fireplace and arched my back over the metal grate. I looked across the room at my mother cooking in the kitchen. I watched Oliver and his cousin run around a corner, their socks slipping on the floor. My father sat down in a chair in the living room. My back hot from the fire, I moved to a chair near him.

"How are you?" I asked.

"Good!" he said. "Have you read this?" He held up the book he was reading, *Chroma* by Derek Jarman.

"I gave that to you, remember?" I said. "It's one of my favorite books."

"Oh! I have a lot of thoughts about it!" he said.

"I've been meaning to ask you. Are you working on your opus?"

"No," he said. "I got to eighteen thousand words. But I can't fabricate a persona. I had one: the dying man. Now with the new diagnosis I don't. So I stopped."

He looked so pleased to have beaten death. Only he hadn't necessarily. I'd been in that doctor's office. The doctor didn't say he was cured, only that the immunotherapy had shrunk his tumors by half and that many outcomes were now possible. As a "long-term responder" to the treatment, my father was now in "a new bin of uncertainty"—in contrast, I supposed, to the old bin of certain imminent death, which wound up not being so certain after all.

My father looked proud of his inability to fabricate a persona, the same way he seemed pleased he could never keep a journal because, he said, he didn't know who he was writing to.

I always kept a diary. I knew who I was writing to: Diary. I apologized to Diary when I didn't write enough. I asked Diary if Diary could believe that at a sixth-grade party none other than George Mitchell had asked me to dance. Then again, I will personify anything that stays still long enough. I apologize to a table if I bump into it.

My father was full of excitement that he and my mother would be flying in a couple of days to Madrid to look at Diego Velázquez paintings at the Prado. Steve Martin was taking them. My father was sharing one of his favorite observations about the magic of private air travel, which he'd experienced just once before, also with Steve Martin. He began to say something I'd heard him say at least a dozen times: "It's like being poured from one champagne glass into another."

Oliver, who'd sat down near us a few minutes earlier, got up in the middle of this recitation and headed to the kitchen to see what my mother was up to.

"Hey!" my father said to him. "I'm talking!"

"He's heard it before," I said.

During dinner, my father left the dinner table to go to his office to smoke. About fifteen minutes later he returned, seeming cheerful. "Steve emailed. He asked me if he could record me when we're in Spain."

"What did you tell him?" I asked.

"My first reaction was no, but then I thought, *Why not?* I said yes."

When I'd asked if I could record his Frick tour, he'd told me that his tours were a *"you had to be there* kind of thing." I knew it wouldn't be the last time my father showed a preference for his friends, nor the last time I would feel hurt by it. It was our routine. I saw that clearly as he sat smiling by the firelight, excited about his trip. I could get mad every time or I could try to stop being so surprised.

When they returned from Spain, my father sent as much as he'd gotten done of his memoir to his editor at the *New Yorker*. She cut the twenty-three-thousand-word document down to a nine-thousand-word essay the online editors titled "The Art of Dying." It included stories from his life and his thoughts on death: "I used to fear the embarrassment of dying youngish, letting people natter sagely, 'He smoked, you know.' But at seventy-seven I'm into the actuarial zone of fatal this, that, and the other thing: the winners' circle."

The essay, published in the issue dated two days before Christmas, was brave and beautiful, a tour de force of an apologia. I noticed that his editor had given it a shape. And to this final reckoning with life, she'd suggested he add more about his family. Didn't he have a grandson? I searched the original twenty-three-thousand-word version of his story, the one he'd turned in, for the names Oliver, Neal, and Blake. None appeared.

The final version included a new story about the ballgame we attended. It mentioned that Oliver had caught a T-shirt from the T-shirt cannon. A paragraph about me made it into the final, too. My father took what I'd told him that day in the apartment—that I always felt he never found me interesting—and used it in his story:

My daughter Ada has told me that she spent years in her childhood trying to interest me. I hadn't noticed. She was sixteen when I got sober. She said, "Let's see if I get this straight. NOW you want to be my Dad?" It took a lot of time and change and is still underway. I don't know if it's a consolation prize for Ada, or what it is, that she turned out to be fantastically interesting.

He also said in the story something I'd always felt but never heard him articulate: "I think off and on about people I love, but I think about writing all the time."

My inbox immediately began filling up with emails congratulating me on having such a terrific father. One editor told me she envied my having a parent who in the face of death had found such a "genius peace." Several fellow writers wrote me long emails about how much they admired my father's brilliant style—how, again, he was AMAZING, and THE BEST. The article was about his impending death, but most of these emails offered me not condolences but praise.

A bookstore owner I knew wrote and said he was thrilled by a rumor he'd heard about my father writing a book about Frank O'Hara. He said there was no better person for the job. (The source of the rumor: a recent *New York Times* profile of me in which I'd mentioned that I was planning to do something with the tapes I'd found.)

I was at the supermarket with Neal and Oliver when I felt my phone vibrate. I looked down and saw an email from a woman I'd interviewed for my Gen X book. The email was full of lavish praise for my father's essay, and it ended with an unironic "What a dad!"

My heart rate sped up. I had trouble catching my breath. I left Neal and Oliver to check out while I went outside and gulped parking-lot air. I looked at my arms to make sure I wasn't actually disappearing, turning translucent, like ghosts in movies.

The following week, as Jason and I sat in an off-Broadway theater waiting for a play to start, I told him that the emails about my fantastic genius father were starting to drive me crazy.

"No!" Jason said. "This is seriously great! It's like on *Law and Order*. You can talk about anything you want from your childhood now because *he opened the door, your honor! My evidence is now admissible!*"

My friend Asia said I should write a rebuttal to the essay, like Liz Phair's song-by-song response to the Rolling Stones' *Exile on Main Street*. She said there was a long-overdue conversation that should happen between men of his generation and their daughters. She said it should include the line "I'm good at things, too, you know."

I thought of the scene in which the new wife in *Rebecca* finally asserts herself with the housekeeper and says, "I am Mrs. de Winter now."

But I didn't feel so self-possessed. I'd worked hard to become my own person, even changed my name. But now, weeks before the publication of what people kept saying would be my "breakthrough" book, I was back to being nothing more than a great man's daughter.

And I was tired.

In the span of six months, Neal's father had died unexpectedly of a stroke, my father had been diagnosed with stage-four lung cancer, my childhood home had been destroyed in a fire, and my grandmother had gone into hospice. I felt hexed. I thought of how Maureen had implied that I had so much going for me and that if I pursued the Frank O'Hara book, bad things would happen. I wondered if this was what she'd meant.

At my regular poker game, my friend Matthew delivered his usual patter as he dealt a hand of seven-card stud high-low: "Looks like Dan's going low with a seventy-five . . . Abbott, two queens, high . . . Ada . . ." Looking at the garbage sitting in front of me, he said, "Ada's going another way." That became my euphemism for 2019: another way. As the terrible year came to an end I thought, *Well, at least 2020 is bound to be better.*

Chapter 33

Nine days into 2020, my grandmother, who'd been living the past year at a nursing home near my aunt Ann in the Catskills, died. My father went to be there with her in her final hours, and it was a moment of redemption for him and his siblings. Ann had struggled to forgive my father for his eulogy of her son sixteen years earlier. About my cousin, the closest thing I had to a brother, my father delivered a rambling monologue about life and poetry and suicide that included the line "little fucker took himself out."

Another sibling was still mad that my father had left his three sisters and one brother at my grandfather's deathbed vigil with the farewell line "Some of us have jobs to get back to." (All had sacrificed to be there. Ann was an accountant, and it was tax season.)

He was my ride home, so I'd left with him. Moments before my grandfather died, he opened his eyes and looked at everyone assembled around his deathbed—four of his five children, several of his grandchildren. But he did not see my father or me. At that moment, we were being stopped by a policeman on the Taconic State Parkway for speeding back to Manhattan.

So everyone was glad my father was handling this death better.

The day after my grandmother died, Neal and Oliver and I went to meet my parents for dinner at a restaurant upstate. My mother arrived first. On his way there, my father drove off the road into a ditch. There was snow on the ground, but that wasn't why. He'd just overshot the turn in the darkness and found himself unable to get back onto the road. A car stopped for him and two men in suits got out. They were—of course they were—morticians. They helped him call us. Neal volunteered to drive to where he was to wait with him for the tow truck. In the meantime, my mother and I drank martinis and chatted with Oliver about school. Less than an hour later, Neal and my father arrived at the restaurant together.

When my father walked in, his hands were shaking. He said he was rattled from the accident and also from Grammy's death: "She grabbed my head between her hands, and that was her last communication. She was suffering horribly."

Next to me, I felt Oliver tense up. He loved his great-grandmother. Once a month or so we visited her, and they discussed books and Norwegian history. They were also pen pals. I tried to signal to my father that he shouldn't talk around Oliver about Grammy being in pain.

"I'm sure she was at peace," I said. "When Lanny was dying, the hospice nurses told us that the death rattle sounds scary and painful, but it doesn't hurt."

"Oh, no, she suffered *a lot*," my father said.

I said something about one of her best friends, and my mother quipped, "Grammy was nobody's best friend."

Oliver piped up: "She was *my* best friend."

He calls a lot of people his best friend, but I swear he means it every time.

The rest of the dinner, Oliver was a little loopy. He'd felt nauseous in the car and had taken a Dramamine. During the meal my father said to him, with sarcasm: "Well, you're riveting company."

Aside from the two pink-cloud weeks, he hadn't really changed much. Even though he'd been told he was dying and his life's work had burned up in a fire—two jolts to the system that might have caused another man to radically alter his outlook—he was still sometimes engaging, sometimes wounding, and you never knew which you'd get.

Neal said, "It's like if in *The Christmas Carol*, Ebenezer Scrooge woke up the next day and threw open the window and asked what day it was, he heard, "'Why, Christmas Day!' and then said, 'Good to know. Back to work, everyone.'"

At the restaurant, I switched the conversation to Frank O'Hara, still a safe harbor. We talked about a controversial book in which a writer offered a hodgepodge of specious arguments suggesting that O'Hara didn't write one of his more famous poems, in which he talks with the sun about death on Fire Island, where he would later die. The book's author suggests that since the poem was clearly a masterpiece but never seen during O'Hara's lifetime, it must have been forged after his death by Kenneth Koch.

Poet Tony Towle, who knew O'Hara and his typewriter, said that O'Hara definitely did write that poem. Koch's estate and O'Hara's estate both sent their lawyers after the book. It was ultimately still published by a small press but without the quotations of O'Hara's and Koch's material.

My father and I have never liked that particular poem much. We decided it was more likely that O'Hara wrote the poem but didn't circulate it because it was too twee.

"In other news," I said, "my new book seems to be doing okay. It's only been a few days since it came out and it's at number forty-three on Amazon."

"Where's my book?" my father asked.

I picked up my phone and checked. "Number twenty-one thousand," I said.

"That seems good, too!" my mother said.

As we were leaving, Oliver hugged my father and said, "Bye! Sorry I wasn't better company." Then as he walked away, he whistled a happy song.

"And *that* is how you don't become a neurotic Schjeldahl," Neal whispered to me.

A couple of weeks later, as I applied liquid eyeliner in a Virginia hotel room before a reading, I got a call from my agent: my book had just hit the *New York Times* bestseller list. In the preceding decade, several books I'd ghostwritten had made the list, but this was the first bestseller that was all mine. I felt overcome with joy. I called Neal. He put me on speaker so I could hear him and Oliver cheering.

I emailed three author friends who'd already been on the list, and they all wrote right back with lots of exclamation points and all-caps congratulations. Jason told me I should report to the secret bestsellers' club for my smoking-jacket fitting. I emailed my parents to tell them the news. My mother wrote back a lovely note about how much I deserved it and how proud she was. My father responded with an email of one word: "Zoom!" and then he never said anything else about it.

That was January.

By March, New Yorkers were dying by the thousands of the coronavirus. To keep my parents safe, I moved them out of their East Village sublet and to their place in the Catskills. Neal, Oliver, and I stayed at our house fifteen minutes away from them. Two days into our lockdown, Oliver's well-fed turtle devoured her roommate, a goldfish she'd been living alongside for two years. It didn't seem like a good omen.

To give us all something to look forward to once a week, Neal and I hosted movie nights at our house. At these dinners, Oliver showed his grandparents the planes and tanks he'd built from model kits. We ate dinners in the backyard and then watched movies on a silver projection screen we'd found years earlier at a garage sale—*Defending Your Life, The Lady Eve, Shane*. My father ate giant bowls of popcorn and boxes of movie candy, and in those moments he seemed happy.

I returned to listening to the Frank O'Hara tapes, trying to make something out of them that would be useful to or engaging for somebody. I started writing my own thoughts about the tapes and the fire and the cancer. And as I reflected on my father for hours a day, I realized that I might be more like him than I'd been willing to admit.

My whole childhood, I wished he'd be kinder, more stable, more available. When he finally was, when he stopped drinking, I was too busy. I spent most of my time with another family. When I began writing, I erased his last name and never even asked him how he felt about it. I took his worst moments—learning he would die, seeing his life's work burn—and used them for material.

I was now writing something that he might hate because I was following in his footsteps, trying to put being a writer first. I felt more tenderly toward my father than I had in a while. He was eccentric, but I understood him. If he'd died then, the ending would have been a happy one. I could have mourned him with the belief that I'd wrapped it all up, made peace.

But he did not die then, and so we continued to fight.

One day as we sat outside in the sunshine, my father told me that Spencer had begun learning Sanskrit.

"Wow," I said.

"Yes!" he said, mistaking my shock for enthusiasm. "Spencer just keeps expanding his erudition in all directions!"

I looked at him smiling at the thought of his smart best friend, and I thought back to when I'd told him, when I was twenty, that I was so good at Sanskrit translating that a professor had offered to help me obtain a fast-tracked and subsidized Asian Studies doctorate. I'd thought he'd be pleased. I'd already gotten a mostly free ride to college. Now it looked like I could get a PhD, too.

He'd looked disappointed and spat out: "So you're going to be a fucking *academic?*" with the repulsion Silent Generation fathers reserved for their hippie children's resolve to tune in and drop out. Then he slammed a kitchen cupboard.

Thinking it would win him over, I'd printed out a translation I'd done of which I was particularly proud. It was of a poem that was thousands of years old. When I finally got him to look at it, he only had one comment, about my adjective choice in a verse about a palace: "Rooftops can't really be *arresting*, can they?"

Someone looking at us from outside as he talked about Spencer's illustrious Sanskrit scholarship would have seen a father and daughter spending time together on a beautiful day. I maintained the illusion by not flinging my cup into the air, screaming, and running to my car.

After all, no one, I felt, would feel sympathy for me. There's no DSM-5 entry for preferring your friend to your child, no mandatory sentencing minimums. I was overreacting. And yet I felt a little like we were in a dumb modern production of *King Lear* and thought of what Frank O'Hara said: "Anyone who chose Goneril and Regan deserved what Lear got."

Then I remembered that the play didn't end so well for Cordelia either.

On the phone while I cooked another big dinner, I told my friend Tara how angry my father made me, how as I was making enchiladas for him and the rest of the family, I kept muttering about things my father had said.

She said that no matter how anyone else acted, I should continue to do what I knew was the right thing.

"Which is?" I asked.

"Making enchiladas," she said.

Chapter 34

To keep my parents from getting exposed to Covid-19, I tried to give them fewer excuses to leave home. I taught them how to use Skype and Zoom so they could talk with Steve Martin and the St. Marks Place co-op. I brought them dinners. And yet, one afternoon I called over to the house and, yet again, my father told me that my mother was out running errands.

"She's in town every time I call," I said. "I told her I'd make those trips for her so she could stay home safe."

"Hey!" he said. "I go to town too! I went yesterday for cigarettes and root beer and gasoline!"

Not "gas": "gasoline," as if he enjoyed the sound of the whole word, symbol of American freedom, the ability to go where you want, when you want: *gas-o-line*. Stage-four lung cancer, seventy-eight years old, explicit orders from doctors and the governor to stay in, my pleas to be careful—none of it was enough to keep him from doing exactly what he wanted to do, whenever he wanted to do it.

I asked him to give me his next shopping list, and this was it: Ritalin, A&W root beer, 72 percent dark chocolate, and a carton of Marlboro Gold 100s. The wish list of any American teenage boy.

Well, except my thirteen-year-old, Oliver, who found his grandfather's tastes a source of great amusement. As I walked, masked, to the strip-mall cigarette store to pick up Poppa's groceries, Oliver leaned out the window of our parked car and shouted across the lot in a voice he'd cribbed from James Cagney's in *White Heat*: "Ma! Get me my cigs, Ma!"

One night, a thunderstorm caused a blackout and I arrived at my parents' the next morning to find four plastic root beer bottles duct-taped together with dinner candles poking out from the tops, wax everywhere. Rather than use a flashlight, my father had crafted a soda bottle candelabra. It looked like an art installation, or a prop from a horror movie—something discovered by detectives in a killer's lair. As I assessed the contraption, I thought back to all those "genius" emails I'd gotten from his fans. And I felt glad that weeks earlier I'd bought several smoke detectors and hidden them around his house.

The hits kept coming. One night as I cleared the table after dinner at their house, I saw a book I'd given him months earlier sitting in the trash with the food. It was *New York Times* reporter David Carr's memoir *The Night of the Gun*. After getting sober, he goes back and reports out his drug addiction and its fallout, especially the effect it had on his daughters. The title comes from a moment when he's retelling a story about how one night his friend had drawn a gun on him. The friend corrects the record; it was Carr who'd been waving around the gun. And now here was this book in the garbage. I pulled it out of the trash and cleaned it off.

"Did you mean to throw this away?" I said.

"Yeah," my father said, without looking up.

"I gave you this book for Christmas," I said. "I told you that I loved this book, that it meant a lot to me. If you wanted to get rid of it, why wouldn't you do it while I wasn't here? Why not throw it away an hour ago or an hour from now so I wouldn't see it?"

My father seemed confused. Over his shoulder I could see my mother and Neal and Oliver and my parents' friend Scott trying to pretend they weren't listening.

"Oh!" he said. "I didn't mean anything by it. I didn't think about it. It definitely wasn't conscious."

"Then you need to get some *fucking therapy!*" I said—louder than I'd meant to, I guessed, because behind him I saw the others stiffen. I didn't want to cause any more of a scene, so I went into the bathroom to pull myself together.

All this time, I'd thought we had books and writing in common. I was a fool. He loved books in his own way and apart from me. Did we share anything? I clung to Frank O'Hara as the one thing that was undeniably ours, like a religion to which we both adhered, even if we didn't go to church together. But now even that felt like a stretch. *I bet he'd remember if Spencer gave him a book*, I thought.

I went into his office and from the literal ashes of his cigarettes I scooped up several other books that I'd given him off the corner of his desk. I brushed them off and put them in my purse. Then I went back into the main room, where preparations were being made to watch a movie. I made everyone popcorn, putting only the slightest topspin on my father's as I set it down in front of him.

In the days that followed, he did not contact me. I imagined him dying while we were in a fight. People always say that it's important to end on good terms. And I knew that if I were to write something about him, it would need a final chapter. Ideally, he would become a doting grandfather and loving father and, having processed every slight and forgiven them all, I would magnanimously put the past behind me. He would die feeling cared for and seen and I would be there for him and my mother. Spencer would be unreachable, maybe in Europe.

But I'd been trying to give us that storybook ending all year, and where had it gotten me? I'd been working nonstop to do right by him, to tell him I loved him and to help him tie up the loose ends of his work, to protect his legacy, to buy him frozen yogurt, to say heartfelt goodbyes so that if they were the last goodbyes, I could be proud of them. After all that, could I live with "You need fucking therapy" as the last thing I said to him? Could I live with Spencer being the good child, for real this time?

I decided that I could. I'd said everything I had to say. He'd said everything he had to say. That was more than most people get. So what if I couldn't hold his attention. So what if he threw my gifts in the trash? I didn't see how I'd ever fix any of that with him, but I could at least take comfort in the fact that I had broken that particular cycle as a parent. Feminist, Civil Rights activist, and author Audre Lorde said, "As women, we need to examine the ways in which our world can be truly different," and I had.

Blake, who was six when Neal and I met, was now a full-fledged adult. He'd been born to teen parents on food stamps and through years of incredibly hard work was now becoming a doctor of physical therapy. After years of getting to see him only a few times a year when he'd lived with his mom in Texas, we now had him near us. And we could finally see him all the time for museums and Coney Island trips and sitting around eating chips and salsa and laughing.

Oliver, a rising ninth grader, still hugged me every day. I knew his teachers and his friends and how he liked his waffles. Reading with Oliver over the years was one of my favorite things—from *The Foot Book* when he was six months old to *Flora and Ulysses* when he was six (it's about a squirrel who writes poetry, mostly about food) to all the *Harry Potter* books to all the *Young Bond* books. And having listened to classic British novels as audiobooks for years, his accents and vocabulary were ridiculous. He was the only Brooklyn-raised boy I knew who used words like "whinging."

When he was in fifth grade, Oliver and I developed a particular love of a hilarious British book series called *Mr. Gum*, so much so that we decided to write the author a fan letter. We mailed it off to him in care of the publisher. The author wrote back and included a new book as well as his email address. We started exchanging emails, and he said he'd be in New York. He came and spoke at the monthly reading series I organized at Oliver's school library and then I took him out for lunch and on a tour of Bushwick. When Oliver and Neal and I were in London, Mr. Gum, as we privately called him, gave us a thumb drive of all his favorite Prince bootlegs and took us on a tour of Primrose Hill. I had to explain to Oliver that this is not what typically happens when you send a fan letter.

Or maybe it is when you're as open as Oliver is—as ready to love and be loved. When my goddaughter Alice was just a few weeks old, Oliver held her carefully as she slept, and if I ever got a tattoo it would be of that moment.

When I saw my father again a few days after the night of *The Night of the Gun*, at Oliver's fourteenth birthday party, he hovered while I manned the grill. He tried to make small talk, but I realized the reason he was standing so close was that he was hungry. He seized the first hamburger I spatulaed onto the platter. While he ate, I mentioned that it might be a good time to apologize for throwing my favorite book away in front of me and acting like I was overreacting when I said it was weird.

He said he couldn't apologize because if you apologized it meant you'd never do it again, and he knew enough about himself to know that he probably would do something like that again. He told me he'd been thinking about his issues a lot, though, and decided there was evil in him, and—

I cut him off and said in the time it took him to figure out how evil he was he could have driven to Price Chopper and bought me an $8 bouquet of flowers and then we wouldn't have to talk about it again. He said he heard the message loud and clear.

When he came down the driveway a week later for another dinner I was cooking for him, I saw that he was carrying something. I felt a flutter of hope that it was for me. But as he got closer, I saw that what he carried was a bowl of whipped cream my mother had made to go on the dessert.

I stayed mad. I couldn't believe I could feel so much anger toward a seventy-eight-year-old man who weighed 125 pounds. It hurt my sense of myself as a good girl, someone who always took the high road.

As Neal and I took one of our daily lockdown walks together, I fumed.

"I know how you're feeling right now," Neal said. "You're sort of looking forward to when your dad is gone because then you think you'll have your life back and you'll stop thinking about him all the time. But everyone with chronically ill parents thinks things like that. And take it from someone with two dead parents: it doesn't work that way. When someone dies, it just means nothing new happens. It doesn't mean you stop thinking about them or being tormented. In fact, sometimes you think about them more, and you're tormented more, because now you're just left with whatever happened already and there are no more re-dos. So be glad he's still alive."

Midway through the summer, the family I stayed with in high school came over for a socially distant backyard barbecue, bringing with them their three-year-old grandchild—my goddaughter Alice. Watching her running toward me, arms out, I smiled so hard it hurt my face. She and I have loved each other since I first met her when she was a few weeks old. In my backyard, I carried her around on my hip and

brought out boxes of old toys for her to play with. I pointed out animals and flowers and made her a plate of food. Concentrating hard on
the words, she sang me her new favorite song, "Home on the Range":
"Where seldom is heard a discouraging word . . ."

Her voice sounded so much like mine on those bedtime tapes. She
was bright and funny and, like Oliver, had a natural affinity for big
words. She would do great things, I thought, and I would do anything
to help her. I reminded myself that I should continue to give her
books every year and that one day one of them would be *Lunch Poems*.

As the sun set, I watched as she played with the toys I'd brought
out for her. I noticed that her favorites were the miniature toy foods
that I'd been looking for a year and a half earlier when I found the
Frank O'Hara tapes. Searching for this simple thing to make her happy
had given me my own old toy to play with—a Rubik's Cube of voices
and stories that had kept me occupied for hundreds of hours and that
I'd probably be trying to solve for the rest of my life.

Chapter 35

As my aunt Ann sorted out Grammy's effects, she supplied me with box after box of impeccably kept paperwork, and I became the keeper of the Schjeldahl family genealogy records. I'd like to say this is because of my reliability, but the truth was that no one else particularly wanted them.

Among the boxes of papers were folders that Grammy had kept on my father and me. My father had told Ann that he didn't want his, but she didn't want to throw it away, so I took both. My dad's was labeled PETER SCHJELDAHL and mine ADA. His dated back to the 1940s, with Mother's Day cards he'd given her in elementary school, letters from when he'd moved to New York, and clippings of his poetry and articles. Mine contained letters I had sent her over the years, *Austin Chronicle* stories I'd written, and copies of my report cards.

In my father's folder, Grammy included pages of her diary from 1980, when I was four and she and my grandfather threw a birthday party for me and my parents at their Gramercy Park Hotel room. Our birthdays are all in the same week—my mother's March 13, mine March 17, my father's March 20. (Frank O'Hara's true birthday, for the record, is March 27.) My grandparents ordered cake from room service, bought candles and balloons, and decorated the room.

My parents and I arrived "looking happy if a bit scruffy. Ada wearing a tan winter coat several sizes too large, a wool knit scarf, and the knit cap I gave her for Christmas. She had on an old-fashioned-type cotton dress, white tights, and black 'Mary Jane' shoes, and she proceeded to remove socks and shoes immediately and had a happy time romping and coloring in her coloring book . . . Ada wanted to take her gifts home wrapped but was persuaded to open them and we played the dice game a little. While the adults chatted she used up most of the tape to rewrap them . . . What an adorable, bright, and sensitive child!

"Peter looks gaunt and unkempt—hair long, w/beard and mustache. Says he lost 20 pounds when he quit drinking, but they both feel more energetic since they quit. [This was an early, unsuccessful attempt at sobriety.] We feel that he didn't seem very happy—hope we misread him."

In my folder was a letter from my father to his mother dated March 21, 1977. He described me at age one: "Her vocabulary is large but hard to understand; I think she may be speaking Chinese . . . 'Cuteness' department: Ada delighted and awed everyone at the party when her cake was presented. Predictably, she grabbed handfuls of the thick flowered icing. Less predictably, she proceeded to walk around presenting each of her guests with a gob of the stuff. The perfect hostess.

"Work & Worry Department: I keep plugging away at the early stages of the book, which more and more seems an absolutely colossal undertaking. The number of people I'll be obliged to talk to easily exceeds a hundred, and there are mountains of papers and documents to ferret out and study.

"One real worry at this point is O'Hara's sister Maureen, who controls the estate and originally picked me to write the book. She keeps promising cooperation and then withholding it; one of her many fears seems to be that I will treat her brother with something less than complete idolatry. Dealing with her has been driving me nuts. I have the warm support of almost everyone else who knew O'Hara and can only hope that this will help sway her."

He did not sway her, of course, and neither did I, but between the two of us we were able to gather information about Frank O'Hara and transmit it. Between us, it took forty-five years, and this is not the way either of us envisioned it happening, but here we are.

As the pandemic continued month after month, New York City businesses kept shuttering and people kept moving away. I learned that Jimmy Webb, a major figure in the punk history of St. Marks Place, had died of cancer when the *New York Times* called me to comment for his obituary. The *Times* also asked me for a photo of my father for his prewritten obit. When he announced he was dying they teed it up.

When I heard that the Odessa Diner on Avenue A, where I'd had lunch with my father to talk about Frank O'Hara, was closing, I went and got takeout and asked the waiter who'd been there forever if the rumors were true. He said no; they were just closing for renovations. But he'd either been lying or mistaken, because it did close after all.

The Second Avenue corner shop Gem Spa, where my parents bought their newspapers from 1973 to 2019, said they were struggling. I went over and donated a box of books for them to sell and bought a bunch of merch, but they closed, too.

When I went to the city to help Blake move into his new apartment, I walked around our neighborhood in my mask and saw that some windows had been broken and others boarded up. The neighborhood smelled like plywood.

In January, I made my parents vaccine appointments the second they became available and drove them round-trip from upstate to the

Javits Center so they could get their shots. My father said he didn't feel different afterward because life was still nowhere near back to normal. But when I saw the needles go into their arms, I was so relieved I cried.

He was right, though, that nothing really changed, certainly not when it came to him and me. And how much longer did he have to live? Still, no one could say. Nearly two years after his "six months" prognosis, my father was the same as he'd been for most of that time—tired, weak, skeletal, still holed up in his office writing and smoking and talking on the phone to Spencer, taking too much of his prescriptions, and rarely leaving the house.

The last time I was in their apartment, my mother and I stood in the demolished space. From the center of the room, we could see St. Marks Place out the front windows and Ninth Street out the back. In spite of how long it would take to rebuild and how much it would cost, I felt a rising hope. In the empty space that once was my bedroom I thought of all the books I'd read there as a child, the guys I'd slept with in high school, the things I'd written or scotch taped on my walls. Those walls and all their words had been chucked by workmen into dumpsters below.

Maybe one day Oliver or Oliver's children will sleep in that room, or other people's children will. Maybe one day the building will fall down entirely and something else will rise in its place. When that day comes, my father will be gone and I'll be gone, too. Will it matter, anything we did or thought or felt? In Frank O'Hara's "Rhapsody," he describes lying in a hammock on St. Marks Place sorting his poems.

What is worth remembering about Frank O'Hara, about my father, about anyone? What I heard in what Maureen said was that her brother should be known only through his work, with that work occasionally subjected to quiet, measured attention from experts, published in chapbooks and anthologies. I gathered she didn't believe that stories like the ones I'd found on the tapes—gossip, hearsay—had any value at all.

We leave behind more than our work, though. We stay behind in memories people have of us rolling around in the snow on Sixth Avenue, throwing dorm-suite cocktail parties, having food fights with children, swimming in the ocean at night.

I hoped that my father let me have those tapes because, at least on some level, he wanted me to know him in his imperfection. I think of myself as open and generous, but I wouldn't want to expose myself like that—with no editing, no restrictions, without even listening to the interviews first. As a brand-new father, he tried to pay tribute to his favorite writer. When he failed, he admitted it.

He stayed with his family even as most of the men in his circle left theirs. In the end, so what if he didn't know my teachers' names? So what if he's not like the fathers in sappy songs, the kind playing catch with their kids in slow motion on Super 8? Let other fathers sit at the head of the dinner table, drive cars with calm authority, practice moderation. This reckless, mercurial, occasionally mean father gave me New York City, touch-typing, National League baseball, and Frank O'Hara.

My father believes his work is his only legacy. I know he's wrong. Whether or not he values it, my father has done more with his life than write. He had me, for one thing. And one day I will leave behind not only my books but also my son and my stepson and my god-children and my house and the memories held by my friends. I took what I needed from him—a sense of the power and importance of writing—and I added to it a belief that it's possible to be good as well as great.

I can't stop returning to that bedtime tape of my father and me as a baby, the one in which we were both struggling to be heard and seen and loved. How ironic that as two writers we have always had such a hard time making ourselves understood to each other. Just like the figure in O'Hara's "To the Harbormaster," we cast off with such promise; then our ships get tangled in the ropes.

There have been moments when we waved from opposite shores or when, briefly, our boats drew close. After one of our movie nights, my father sent me an email that read:

If I weren't your dad, I'd wish I were. Or your brother or poker buddy or grocer. Anything, to know you.

Reading that, I was moved but also wary. These moments of tenderness are so often like the night we played cards forty years before that meant so much to me but nothing to him. If these flashes of affection were all I ever got, could I let them pat out my rage like a fire blanket? It had to count for something that one morning after a night that seemed like any other, he could say, with poetic economy, what I'd always wanted to hear: he liked having me around.

Perhaps I have been spending so much time with these tapes because they are evidence of something I need to hold onto: In those rare moments when we weren't misunderstanding each other or battling for control, our voices sounded sweet together.

Ada's Bedtime—New York City—11/22/78

PS and A: You take the high road and I'll take the low road and I'll be
    in—
A: Daddy, why do you want that? [Pointing to tape recorder.]
PS: Oh, well, I just thought it'd be nice. I'd like to sing with you.
A: Why?
PS: 'Cause it's fun. . . . Let's try "Loch Lomond" again. Sing it
    together?
A: Yeah.

PS and A: O, you'll take the high road, and I'll take the low road, / and I'll be in Scotland afore ye, / But me and my true love will never meet again / On the bonnie, bonnie banks of Loch Lomond!
PS: Yippee!
A: Yippee!

Bibliography

Ashbery, John. *Self-Portrait in a Convex Mirror.* New York: Penguin, 2009.

Ashton, Dore. *The New York School: A Cultural Reckoning.* New York: Penguin, 1992.

Baraka, Amiri. *The Autobiography of LeRoi Jones.* Chicago: Lawrence Hill Books, 1997.

Berkson, Bill, ed. *Best and Company.* Williamstown, MA: Chapel Press, 1969.

Berkson, Bill. *A Frank O'Hara Notebook.* San Francisco: no place press, 2019.

Berkson, Bill. *Since When: A Memoir in Pieces.* Minneapolis: Coffee House Press, 2018.

Berkson, Bill. *Sudden Address: Selected Lectures 1981–2006.* Berkeley: Cuneiform Press, 2007.

Berkson, Bill, and Joe LeSueur, eds. *Homage to Frank O'Hara.* Berkeley: Creative Arts Book Company, 1980.

Berkson, Bill, and Frank O'Hara. *Hymns of St. Bridget and Other Writings.* Woodacre, CA: The Owl Press, 2001. Also published in a stapled, xeroxed edition by St. Mark's Poetry Project's Adventures in Poetry.

Bollas, Christopher. *The Shadow of the Object: Psychoanalysis of the Unthought Known.* New York: Columbia University Press, 1987.

Broyard, Anatole. *Intoxicated by My Illness: And Other Writings on Life and Death.* New York: Ballantine Books, 2010.

Brossard, Olivier, ed. *Lovers of My Orchards: Writers and Artists on Frank O'Hara.* Montpellier, France: Presses Universitaires de la Méditerranée, 2017.

Burt, Stephen. "Poets of Painting." *Times Literary Supplement,* July 16, 2010.

Byrom, Thomas. "The Poet of the Painters." *Times Literary Supplement*, January 27, 1978.

Caples, Garrett. "Incidents of Travel in New York: The Lives of Frank Lima." In *Incidents of Travel in Poetry*. San Francisco: City Lights, 2015.

Caples, Garrett. "Naked 'Lunch': Behind the Scenes of Frank O'Hara's *Lunch Poems*." PoetryFoundation.org, June 18, 2014.

Carrère, Emmanuel. *Lives Other Than My Own*. New York: Picador, 2012.

Chiasson, Dan. "Fast Company: The World of Frank O'Hara." *New Yorker*, April 7, 2008.

Ciabattari, Jane. "Frank O'Hara: Poet of the *Mad Men* Era." BBC.com, October 21, 2014.

Cifelli, Edward M. *John Ciardi: A Biography*. Fayetteville: University of Arkansas Press, 1997.

Cummings, Paul. "Oral History Interview with Tibor de Nagy." Smithsonian Archives of American Art, March 29, 1976.

Dawson, Fielding. *Delayed: Not Postponed*. Cambridge, MA: Telephone Books, New England Free Press, 1978.

Dery, Mark. *Born to Be Posthumous: The Eccentric Life and Mysterious Genius of Edward Gorey*. New York: Little, Brown, 2018.

Dyer, Geoff. *Out of Sheer Rage: Wrestling with D. H. Lawrence*. New York: North Point Press, 1998.

Elledge, Jim. *Frank O'Hara: To Be True to a City*. Ann Arbor: University of Michigan Press, 1990.

Epstein, Andrew. "Vincent Warren, Love of Frank O'Hara's Life, Passes Away at 79." *Locus Solus*, November 11, 2017.

Factor, Donald, and Anthony Linick, eds. *Nomad New York*. London: Villiers Publications, 1962.

Fein, Skylar. "Eulogy for Frank O'Hara: Pop Art and the Queer Death Drive." Contemporary Arts Museum Houston, Houston, TX. July 7, 2016. YouTube video, 26:34. https://www.youtube.com/watch?v=bPTlnUu_nms.

Feldman, Alan. *Frank O'Hara: Twayne's United States Authors Series*. Boston: Twayne Publishers, 1979.

Flinn, Mary. "An Interview with Peter Schjeldahl." *Blackbird Archive: An Online Journal of Literature and the Arts* 3, no. 1 (Spring 2004).

Foley, Dylan. "An Interview with the Greenwich Village Poet and Hellraiser Brigid Murnaghan, Bleecker Street, May 2014. *The Last Bohemians* (blog), January 1, 2019.

Gabriel, Mary. *Ninth Street Women*. New York: Little, Brown, 2018.

Goldstein, Richard. *Helluva Town: The Story of New York City During World War II*. New York: Free Press, 2010.

Gooch, Brad. *City Poet: The Life and Times of Frank O'Hara*. New York: Harper Perennial, 1993.

Gornick, Vivian. *The Odd Woman and the City: A Memoir*. Reprint edition. New York: Farrar, Straus and Giroux, 2016.

Gosse, Edmund. *Father and Son*. New York: Oxford University Press, 2009.

Gruen, John. *The Party's Over Now*. New York: Viking Press, 1972.

Hamilton, Ian. *In Search of J. D. Salinger*. New York: Random House, 1988.

Hendrix, Jenny. "The Mystery Behind Frank O'Hara's Most Famous Poem." *New Republic*, December 10, 2012.

Hogan, Emma. "Uncertain Intimacy." *Times Literary Supplement*, February 18, 2011.

Isherwood, Christopher. *Kathleen and Frank: The Autobiography of a Family*. New York: Farrar, Straus and Giroux, 1971.

Kane, Daniel. *Don't Ever Get Famous: Essays on New York Writing after the New York School*. Champaign, IL: Dalkey Archive Press, 2006.

Kane, Daniel. *"Do You Have a Band?" Poetry and Punk Rock in New York City*. New York: Columbia University Press, 2017.

Katz, Ada, ed. *Eight Begin: Artists' Memories of Starting Out*. Waterville, Maine: Colby Museum of Art, 2014.

King, Martha. *Outside/Inside . . . Just Outside the Art World's Inside*. Buffalo, NY: BlazeVOX Books, 2018.

Koch, Katherine. "Love and Irony: Postcards from a Child of the New York School." *Hanging Loose*, no.102 (2013): 4.

Koch, Kenneth. *The Art of the Possible: Comics Mainly Without Pictures*. Brooklyn, NY: Soft Skull Press, 2004.

Koch, Kenneth. *Making Your Own Days: The Pleasures of Reading and Writing Poetry*. New York: Scribner, 1998.

Koch, Kenneth. *Selected Poems*. Edited by Ron Padgett. New York: Library of America, 2007.

Lally, Michael, ed. *None of the Above: New Poets of the USA*. Trumansburg, NY: Crossing Press, 1976.

LeSueur, Joe. *Digressions on Some Poems by Frank O'Hara*. New York: Farrar, Straus and Giroux, 2003.

LeSueur, Joe. *You Were a Bastard for Being So Fucking Good in Bed or The Unmentionable*. New York: Chelsea Copy Press, 1982.

Libby, Anthony. "O'Hara on the Silver Range." *Contemporary Literature* 17, no. 2 (Spring 1976): 240–62.

Malcolm, Janet. *The Silent Woman: Sylvia Plath and Ted Hughes*. New York: Knopf, 1995.

Maymudes, Victor, and Jacob Maymudes. *Another Side of Bob Dylan: A Personal History on the Road and off the Tracks.* New York: St. Martin's Press, 2014.

Mendelson, Edward. *Moral Agents: Eight Twentieth-Century American Writers.* New York: New York Review Books, 2015.

Meyer, Thomas. "Glistening Torsos, Sandwiches, and Coca-Cola." *Parnassus: Poetry in Review* 6, no. 1 (Fall/Winter 1977): 241–57.

Moore, Richard O. *USA: Poetry, Frank O'Hara.* Thirteen/WNET New York, March 5, 1966.

Morgan, Bill. *The Beat Generation in New York: A Walking Tour of Jack Kerouac's City.* San Francisco: City Lights, 1997.

O'Hara, Frank. *Art Chronicles, 1954–1966.* New York: George Braziller, 1975.

O'Hara, Frank. *Belgrade, November 19, 1963.* New York: St. Mark's Poetry Project's Adventures in Poetry, undated.

O'Hara, Frank. *The Collected Poems of Frank O'Hara.* Edited by Donald Allen. Berkeley: University of California Press, 1995.

O'Hara, Frank. *Early Writing.* Edited by Donald Allen. San Francisco: Grey Fox Press, 1977.

O'Hara, Frank. *The End of the Far West (11 Poems).* Unidentified press and undated.

O'Hara, Frank. *Lament and Chastisement.* New York: St. Mark's Poetry Project, 1977.

O'Hara, Frank. *Lunch Poems. The Pocket Poets Series, number 19.* San Francisco: City Lights, 1964.

O'Hara, Frank. *Meditations in an Emergency.* 2nd ed. New York: Grove Press, 1967.

O'Hara, Frank. "A Memoir." In *Larry Rivers.* Waltham, MA: Brandeis University, 1965.

O'Hara, Frank. *In Memory of My Feelings.* New York: Museum of Modern Art, 2005.

O'Hara, Frank. *Nakian.* Garden City, NY: Museum of Modern Art, Doubleday, 1966.

O'Hara, Frank. *New Spanish Painting and Sculpture.* Garden City, NY: Museum of Modern Art, Doubleday, undated.

O'Hara, Frank. *Odes.* New York: Poets Press, 1969.

O'Hara, Frank. *Oranges.* New York: Angel Hair Books, undated.

O'Hara, Frank. *Poems Retrieved.* Edited by Donald Allen. San Francisco: Grey Fox Press, 1977.

O'Hara, Frank. *Second Avenue.* New York: Corinth Press, 1969.

O'Hara, Frank. *Selected Plays.* New York: Full Court Press, 1978.

BIBLIOGRAPHY

O'Hara, Frank. *Selected Poems*. Edited by Mark Ford. New York: Alfred A. Knopf, 2008.

O'Hara, Frank. *Standing Still and Walking in New York*. Edited by Donald Allen. San Francisco: Grey Fox Press, 1983.

O'Hara, Frank, et al. *Artists' Theatre New York*. New York: Grove Press, 1960.

Padgett, Ron, ed. *Painter Among Poets: The Collaborative Art of George Schneeman*. New York: Granary Books, 2004.

Padgett, Ron. *Ted: A Personal Memoir of Ted Berrigan*. Great Barrington, MA: Figures, 1993.

Perloff, Marjorie. "'The Ecstasy of Always Bursting Forth!': Rereading Frank O'Hara." In Frank O'Hara, *Selected Poems*. Edited by Mark Ford. New York: Alfred A. Knopf, 2008.

Perloff, Marjorie. *Frank O'Hara: Poet Among Painters*. New York: George Braziller, 1977.

Perloff, Marjorie. "From Image to Action: The Return of Story in Postmodern Poetry." *Contemporary Literature* 23, no. 4 (Fall 1982): 411.

Perloff, Marjorie. "Rereading Frank O'Hara's *Lunch Poems* After Fifty Years." *Poetry* 205, no. 4 (January 2015): 383–91.

Porter, Fairfield. "Poets and Painters in Collaboration." *Evergreen Review* 5, no. 20 (September–October 1961): 121–5.

Rivers, Larry, with Arnold Weinstein. *What Did I Do? The Unauthorized Autobiography*. New York: HarperCollins, 1992.

Roffman, Karin. *The Songs We Know Best: John Ashbery's Early Life*. New York: Farrar, Straus, and Giroux, 2017.

Roiphe, Katie. *The Violet Hour: Great Writers at the End*. New York: Dial Press, 2016.

Rorem, Ned. *Knowing When to Stop: A Memoir*. New York: Simon and Schuster, 1994.

Rosner, Elizabeth. *Survivor Café: The Legacy of Trauma and the Labyrinth of Memory*. New York: Counterpoint, 2017.

Sandler, Irving. *The New York School: The Painters and Sculptors of the Fifties*. New York: Harper and Row, 1978.

Sarrazin, Albertine. *Astragal*. Translated by Patsy Southgate. New York: New Directions, 2013.

Schiff, Harris. *One More Beat*. New York: Accent Editions, 2011.

Schjeldahl, Peter. "Farewell Column." *Village Voice*, October 27, 1998.

Schneiderman, Josh, ed. *The Correspondence of Kenneth Koch and Frank O'Hara 1955–1956, Part I and II*. CUNY Poetics Document Initiative, Series I, no. 2 (Winter 2009).

Schuyler, James. *Freely Espousing*. Garden City, NY: Doubleday, 1969.

Smith, Alexander, Jr. *Frank O'Hara: A Comprehensive Bibliography*. New York: Garland Publishing, 1979.

Storr, Robert. "On Art and Artists: Peter Schjeldahl." *Profile* 3, no. 4 (July 1983).

Strausbaugh, John. *The Village*. New York: Ecco, 2013.

Thomas, Louisa. "The Art of Biography No. 4: Hermione Lee." *Paris Review*, no. 205 (Summer 2013).

Tuchman, Maurice. *New York School: The First Generation*. Greenwich, CT: New York Graphic Society, 1965.

Updike, John. "One Cheer for Literary Biography." *New York Review of Books*, February 4, 1999.

Vendler, Helen. "The Virtues of the Alterable." *Parnassus: Poetry in Review* 1, no. 1 (Fall/Winter 1972): 5–20.

Wakefield, Dan. *New York in the 50s*. New York: Houghton Mifflin, 1992.

Waldman, Anne. "A Phonecall from Frank O'Hara." In *Helping the Dreamer: Selected Poems, 1966–1988*. Minneapolis: Coffee House Press, 1989.

Waldman, Anne, ed. *The World Anthology: Poems from the St. Mark's Poetry Project*. Indianapolis: Bobbs-Merrill Company, 1969.

Ward, Geoff. *Statutes of Liberty: The New York School of Poets*. New York: Palgrave Macmillan, 1993.

Watkin, William. *In the Process of Poetry: The New School and the Avant-Garde*. Lewisburg, PA: Bucknell University Press, 2001.

Wootten, William. "So Good They Wrote It Twice." *Times Literary Supplement*, June 4, 2004.

Selected Frank O'Hara Poems

"Ave Maria"

"Poem [Lana Turner has collapsed!]"

"Having a Coke with You"

"The Day Lady Died"

"Steps"

"To the Harbormaster"

Also a Poet Mixtape

"Canary" — Liz Phair

"Daddy Needs a Drink" — Drive-By Truckers

BIBLIOGRAPHY

"La Vie de Bohème" — Frenchy and the Punk

"The Best Day" — Taylor Swift

"Fade Like a Shadow" — KT Tunstall

"That's My Job" — Conway Twitty

"More Adventurous" — Rilo Kiley

"That's Just the Way That I Feel" — Purple Mountains

"Frank O'Hara" — Sea Wolf

"I Love You, Yes I Do" — Tab Hunter

"V.G.I." — Julie Ruin

"Ghost!" — Kid Cudi

"We Just Disagree" — Dave Mason

"Your Generation" — Generation X

"Dirty Fingers" — Lindsay Ellyn

"Real Friends" — Kanye West

"Don't Call" — Desire

"By This River" — Brian Eno

"He Didn't Say" — Mecca Normal

"Frank O'Hara Hit" — Chelsea Light Moving

Notes

3 "Everything about O'Hara Peter Schjeldahl, "Frank O'Hara: He Made Things and People Sacred," *Village Voice*, August 11, 1966.

3 "EXHIBITIONS AIDE AT MODERN ART "Frank O'Hara, Museum Curator, 40," *New York Times*, July 26, 1966.

4 Now in New York, Somewhat more famously, Gary Simmons accompanied Wayland Flowers and his puppet, Madame.

5 "He seems to have Peter Schjeldahl, "O'Hara—Art Sustained Him," *New York Times*, March 3, 1974. Years later, my father told Steve Martin in an interview: "I did tumble into clarity when I stopped trying to be John Ashbery and started trying to be Frank O'Hara." Stephanie Murg, "Steve Martin Talks Art with Peter Schjeldahl at New Yorker Festival," Adweek.com, October 7, 2011.

5 "In many respects, Roger Kimball, "A Very Sixties Person: Peter Schjeldahl on Art," *New Criterion*, November 1991.

6 One book from 1979 Alan Feldman, *Frank O'Hara: Twayne's United States Authors Series* (Boston: Twayne Publishers, 1979), p. 11.

9 "cheerful and mannerly." Jay Ruttenberg, "Has Ada Calhoun Just Become the Most Important New Voice on Old New York?" *Village Voice*, October 27, 2015.

12 My father opened it Patsy Southgate, "My Night with Frank O'Hara," in *Homage to Frank O'Hara*, eds. Bill Berkson and Joe LeSueur (Berkeley: Creative Arts Book Company, 1980), 119–21.

15 "Now I am quietly Frank O'Hara, "Mayakovsky," in *Meditations in an Emergency* (New York: Grove Press, 1967), 51.

17 "marks of weakness, "Our Life in Poetry: Frank O'Hara Poetry Reading and Discussion," Philoctetes Center for the Multidisciplinary Study

of the Imagination, Participants: Michael Braziller, Mark Doty, and David Lehman, November 11, 2010. YouTube video, 1:40:31, https://www.youtube.com/watch?v=8Z8sxX8YCMw.

18 **O'Hara got a job** "Frank O'Hara, Lunchtime Poet," MoMA website, https://www.moma.org/calendar/galleries/5147.

18 **a Matisse retrospective.** James Schuyler, "Frank O'Hara: Poet Among Painters (excerpts)," in *Homage to Frank O'Hara*, eds. Bill Berkson and Joe LeSueur (Berkeley: Creative Arts Book Company, 1980), 82.

18 **he became a valuable emissary** O'Hara was painted by Larry Rivers, Alice Neel, John Button, Robert Motherwell, Fairfield Porter, Jane Freilicher, Elaine de Kooning, Grace Hartigan, and Alex Katz.

20 **including a night guard** Kenward Elmslie provided a similar account of O'Hara's sex exploits in an interview with *Gay Sunshine* magazine. Winston Leyland, ed., *Gay Sunshine Interviews*, vol. 2 (University of Virginia: Gay Sunshine Press, 1978), 103.

22 **All lyric poems are narcissistic** Charles Simic, "How to Peel a Poem," *Harper's* 299, no. 1792 (September 1999), 152–5.

23 **He overheard O'Hara** Joe LeSueur, *Digressions on Some Poems by Frank O'Hara*, (New York: Farrar, Straus and Giroux, 2003), 229.

27 **"a voice that often reminded me** Ron Padgett, "Six Memories of Frank," in *Homage to Frank O'Hara*, eds. Bill Berkson and Joe LeSueur (Berkeley: Creative Arts Book Company, 1980), 133.

30 **"Even casual acquaintances** Martha King, *Outside/Inside . . . Just Outside the Art World's Inside* (Buffalo, NY: BlazeVOX Books, 2018), 217.

32 **George Montgomery had a long life** "George Montgomery, Poet, Photographer and Curator, 73," *New York Times*, April 14, 1997.

35 **"that the time is not yet ripe** Marjorie Perloff, *Frank O'Hara: Poet Among Painters* (New York: George Braziller, 1977), iv (by my count—the introduction pages aren't numbered). Elsewhere Perloff referred to my father as a "New York antipoet" and O'Hara cultist. Marjorie Perloff, "Poetry Chronicle, 1970–1971," (Albuquerque: University of New Mexico Press, 2019), 33.

35 **The largest void** Fragments of letters have been published here and there, as in Brad Gooch's *City Poet* and Andrew Epstein's *Beautiful Enemies*. On the anniversary of *Lunch Poems*, a few notes between O'Hara and his editor, Lawrence Ferlinghetti, appeared in the *Paris Review*. They're dated 1963–65 and reveal that O'Hara wrote his own jacket copy and picked the book's colors—his favorites—orange and blue. Nicole Rudick, "Lunch Poem Letters," *Paris Review*, June 11, 2014.

35 **I think of this piece**   Ron Padgett, *Collected Poems* (Minneapolis: Coffee House Press, 2013), 117. Reprinted with permission of Ron Padgett and Coffee House Press.

36 **In Manhattan, Padgett wound up**   Padgett said that parties were often held at Bill Berkson's apartment on Fifty-Seventh Street or at Morris Golde's apartment on West Eleventh, and that Jane Freilicher was the wittiest person he'd ever met.

38 **He decided that he**   Allen Ginsberg told them they should also publish Gregory Corso and Robert Creeley.

40 **Two chapbooks contain**   Josh Schneiderman, ed., *The Correspondence of Kenneth Koch and Frank O'Hara 1955–1956, Part I and II*. CUNY Poetics Document Initiative, Series I, no. 2 (Winter 2009).

42 **"for hay is dried-up grass**   Kenneth Koch, "Mending Sump" (1950), in *The New American Poetry 1945–1960*, ed. Donald Allen (New York: Grove Press, 1960), 229. Used with the permission of the Kenneth Koch estate.

43 *New American Poetry 1945–1960.*   Not to be confused with the more academic anthology of poetry edited by Donald Hall that came out around the same time.

44 **Marcel Proust wrote:**   Marcel Proust, *Time Regained* (London: Chatto and Windus, 1931), 240.

46 **Cronin's**   Cronin's was a popular Harvard bar at the time. When Osgood and O'Hara were drinking there, beer cost ten cents. "Fifteen Cent Beer Price Threatened," *Harvard Crimson*, November 10, 1950.

47 **Osgood decided that O'Hara**   Larry Osgood died in December 2018, just a couple of months after I found those tapes in my parents' basement. According to his obituary, he left behind two nieces and would be remembered as "a lover of music, literature, dogs, and great friends." He'd written plays and essays and taken a number of trips to the Arctic by kayak. Dapson Chestney Funeral Home online obituary, dapsonchestney.com/obituary/Lawrence-Osgood. Accessed May 14, 2020.

53 **"One of the most agreeable children**   Christopher Isherwood, *Liberation: Diaries*, vol. 3, 1970–1983 (New York: Harper Perennial, 2013), 638.

66 **"I remember one very cold**   Joe Brainard, *I Remember* (New York: Granary Books, 2001), 20.

68 **When Vincent Warren left**   Frank O'Hara, "Variations on Saturday," in *The Collected Poems of Frank O'Hara*, ed. Donald Allen (Berkeley: University of California Press, 1995), 378.

68 **"One summer, in the late fifties,**   Pssst, John Gruen: You said "young" twice. John Gruen, *The Party's Over Now* (New York: Viking Press, 1972), 147.

70 **"the ever-present third man** William Grimes, "Bill Berkson, Poet and Art Critic of '60s Manhattan In-Crowd, Dies at 76," *New York Times*, June 22, 2016.

70 **rave review in the** *Washington Post* Troy Jollimore, "Bill Berkson's *A Frank O'Hara Notebook* Is a Magical Artifact from Another Era," *Washington Post*, August 8, 2019. Used with permission of the Bill Berkson estate.

71 **A woman has fallen** From Bill Berkson, "Costanza," in *Expect Delays* (Minneapolis: Coffee House Press, 2014), 11.

72 **B. kept apparently saying something** Lisa Birman, ed., *Dearest Annie: You Wanted a Report on Berkson's Class: Letters from Frances LeFevre to Anne Waldman* (Brooklyn, NY: Hanging Loose Press, 2016), 22.

72 **"unthinking worship** Lisa Birman, ed., *Dearest Annie: You Wanted a Report on Berkson's Class: Letters from Frances LeFevre to Anne Waldman* (Brooklyn, NY: Hanging Loose Press, 2016), 36.

74 **"too hip for the squares** John Ashbery said that O'Hara was "the first modern poet to realize that the question was there, waiting to be asked, and he formulated it in terms of the highest beauty." (The question: "Can art do this? Is this really happening?") John Ashbery, "Frank O'Hara's Question," *New York Herald Tribune: Book Week* 4, no. 3, September 25, 1966. Found in John Ashbery, *Selected Prose* (Ann Arbor: University of Michigan Press, 2005), 81–83.

74 **In 1985, my father wrote** "Hard Times for Poets," *New York Times*, September 15, 1985.

75 **By contrast, Kenneth Koch,** My father's interview with Kenneth Koch didn't yield much, except for Koch's account of discovering O'Hara's poetry: "I don't think I wrote a poem for the next three months that didn't have some word in it like 'aspirin tablet' or 'jujube' or 'doorknob' or one of those early Frank O'Hara words. That's why when you asked me which of Frank's poems I liked the best, it's very hard to get those early ones out of my mind. Because they were like my first love, you know?"

75 **The executorship team** The executorship team: Ron Padgett, Jordan Davis, and Justin Jamail.

80 **Philip is full of details** Some background: Frank O'Hara, born in 1926, was the oldest of three. He and his brother, Philip, born in 1933, and sister, Maureen, born in 1937, were the children of Russell and Katherine (Kay) O'Hara, middle-class, suburban Irish Americans. In Baltimore, Russell sold Stetson hats. When his great-uncle, J. Frank Donahue, died, he returned to Grafton to take over the family business, along with his younger brother, Leonard.

83   **He said he used to lay awake**   In his memoir of the war, *Lament and Chastisement: A Travelogue of War and Personality*, O'Hara bemoaned the deaths in war of architects, scientists, and musicians. Frank O'Hara, *Early Writing*, ed. Donald Allen (San Francisco: Grey Fox Press, 1977), 128.

86   **The ensuing melodrama**   Philip fondly remembered the de Koonings, the Motherwells, Joe LeSueur, and J. J. Mitchell. But many of the others, he said, only seemed to care about their own grief.

87   **He died with no will.**   Brad Gooch, *City Poet: The Life and Times of Frank O'Hara* (New York: Harper Perennial, 1993), 467.

87   **doctrine of fair use.**   Fair use is a murky area. The resources that I found most helpful were a 2021 seminar at the New York Public Library called "The (Copy)right Stuff: Intellectual Property Rights Basics for Researchers," with Kiowa Hammons, the Library's rights clearance manager; and a 2020 Gumshoe Group defamation training hosted by Ava Lubell, NYC local journalism attorney for the Cornell Law School First Amendment Clinic. According to the Center for Media and Social Impact's Code of Best Practices for Fair Use for Poetry, produced in January 2011 and available at cmsimpact.org, "under fair use, a critic discussing a published poem or body of poetry may quote freely as justified by the critical purpose."

88   **Frank gave me this poem.**   "Winston Leyland Interviews Ned Rorem," in *Gay Sunshine Interviews*, vol. 2 (San Francisco: Gay Sunshine Press, 1982), 205.

88   **On one of my father's two trips**   Bill Berkson, *A Frank O'Hara Notebook* (San Francisco: no place press, 2019).

90   **He didn't fit in**   Mark Dery, *Born to Be Posthumous: The Eccentric Life and Mysterious Genius of Edward Gorey* (New York: Little, Brown, 2018), 71.

91   **"sit down and *tweedle, tweedle, tweedle,***   O'Hara almost always wrote on his typewriter. He struggled to write anything good without it, LeSueur said. Joe LeSueur, *Digressions on Some Poems by Frank O'Hara* (New York: Farrar, Straus and Giroux, 2003), xvi.

92   **Bunny had Hodgkin's disease**   The stories about Bunny Lang are legion. One time she pasted one thousand two-by-three-inch pink notes reading, in black letters, "My name is Stanley and I am a pig" all over Manhattan, anywhere Stanley—a junior executive who she felt had wronged her—was likely to be. She not only put them all over his apartment building and neighborhood but also inside his place of business, including the bathrooms, and his favorite bars and bookstores—even his laundromat. She kept 150 so she could continue mailing them to him for a long time. Alison Lurie, *V. R. Lang: A Memoir* (self-published, 1959), 67–68. The 1959 version of the book about Lang, which I found on eBay with a cover

by Edward Gorey, is more colorful than the one published in 1975 by Random House, which, according to Gorey, was censored by Lang's family. A review of this edition declared, "Eccentricity, in retrospect, seems limited and a little sad . . . [Lang's] magic cannot be conveyed." Sallie Bingham, "V. R. Lang," *New York Times Book Review*, October 26, 1975.

92 **"That's Bunny Lang.**   Andrew Epstein, "'First Bunny Died': Frank O'Hara With, and After, Bunny Lang," *Spoke* 4, 2017.

92 **"a mysteriosabelle."**   Frank O'Hara, "A Mexican Guitar," in *Meditations in an Emergency*, 2nd ed. (New York: Grove Press, 1967), 28.

92 **And this Security,**   Alison Lurie, *V. R. Lang: A Memoir* (self-published, 1959), 68. The Ben Jonson poem appears in Robert Anderson, ed., *The Works of the British Poets*, vol. 4 (Edinburgh: John and Arthur Arch, et al. 1795), 571.

94 **Down, Gordon, down!**   This Gordon was probably Gordon Boyd, a young artist who was part of the artists and writers set at the University of Tulsa in the late 1950s.

94 **He spent his final years**   Mel Gussow, "Edward Gorey, Artist and Author Who Turned the Macabre into a Career, Dies at 75," *New York Times*, April 17, 2000.

94 **Usually, the Yankees were winners**   In 1962, the New York Mets' inaugural season, the sportswriter Roger Angell wrote: "This was a new recognition that perfection is admirable but a trifle inhuman . . . there is more Met than Yankee in every one of us." Roger Angell, "The Sporting Scene: The 'Go!' Shouters," *New Yorker*, June 16, 1962, 121.

98 *O'Hara's appointment books?*   I got a lead that the appointment books might have ended up with Ted Berrigan, but his widow, the poet Alice Notley, and their two sons, the poets Anselm and Eddie Berrigan, told me they'd never seen them. Notley added, "I would definitely have known and would remember. Ted would have worshipped them and made speeches about them, and I would have been awestruck." Alice Notley, email to the author, May 27, 2020.

98 **She says I can keep all the material**   In June 2020, I scanned the letters, most of which were from Fairfield Porter to Robert Dash, and emailed the PDF to Liza Kirwin at the Smithsonian's Archives of American Art, which houses Fairfield Porter's papers. She said she'd love to have them but that by rights the letters, because they were sent to Bob Dash, should be with Dash's papers at Yale. Nancy Kuhl, Curator of Poetry at the Beinecke Rare Book and Manuscript Library, said they would be a great addition to Dash's archive. You can visit them there now.

100 **There is no place in America**   Alice Notley, "The Prophet," in *Grave of Light: New and Selected Poems 1970–2005* (Middletown, CT: Wesleyan University Press, 2006), 102. Used with the permission of Alice Notley.

101 **"Gee, thanks."**   Irving Sandler, *Goodbye to Tenth Street* (Seattle: Pleasure Boat Studio: A Literary Press, 2018), 77.

102 **Mitchell Paints a Picture."**   Irving Sandler, "Mitchell Paints a Picture," *ARTnews*, October 1957. Reprinted at ARTnews.com, November 5, 2012.

104 **He was witty and charming,**   A *TLS* essay calls "The Day Lady Died" "a poem about not knowing people . . . The poem's one moment of unanimity is at the finish, a tribute to the singer and a premonition of death, hers and everyone else's." Michael Hoffman, "Feeling Good about New York City," *Times Literary Supplement*, December 13, 1991.

104 **"There is always some death**   Bill Berkson, "Frank O'Hara at 30," in *Sudden Address: Selected Lectures 1981–2006* (Berkeley: Cuneiform Press, 2007), 91.

104 **Helen Vendler wrote:**   Helen Vendler, "The Virtues of the Alterable," *Parnassus: Poetry in Review* 1, no. 1 (1972): 6.

105 **"We fail to recognize**   Letter from Sparrow to the author, November 23, 2019.

109 **Mondrian apparently**   Amei Wallach interview with Elaine de Kooning, November 1, 1986, 36.

109 **or the time in 1951**   Amei Wallach interview with Elaine de Kooning, March 17, 1988, 11.

110 **as-told-to interview with Franz Kline**   Frank O'Hara, "Franz Kline Talking," in *Evergreen Review Reader 1957–1966* (New York: Arcade Publishing, 2011).

110 **"To be right**   De Kooning died in 1997, but another painter of the period, Jasper Johns, is alive, and a friend gave me his email address. I wrote and asked what he thought about Frank O'Hara's legacy. He wrote back: "As a participant in the areas of poetry, art, and music Frank was of course an important figure during the time in which I knew him. His generosity to younger artists was well known and benefitted many. His interest in my painting was a boost to my own confidence and I valued his attempts to broaden my interest in poets of the period. I can't remember if he told me that he never took notes when he interviewed artists but wrote down the material when he got home. I know that he said that he had done this when he interviewed Franz Kline. He said that he had omitted from the interview that Franz had said, 'To be right is the most boring thing in the world!' " Jasper Johns, email to the author, July 15, 2019.

110 **"an enigma,** Frank O'Hara, "Larry Rivers, *The Next to Last Confederate Soldier*," in *School of New York: Some Younger Artists*, ed. B. H. Friedman (New York: Grove Press, 1959).

110 **"Larry Rivers is one of the most fascinating** Peter Schjeldahl, "At the Mad Fringes of Art," *New York Times*, November 18, 1979.

112 **"Let's see what a kiss** John Gruen, *The Party's Over Now* (New York: Viking Press, 1972), 141. On this page, Rivers says the same thing to Gruen that he said to my father, about how he likes "boys, girls, animals." In his memoir he describes having sex often with a blue velvet chair. Larry Rivers, "The Chair," in *What Did I Do? The Unauthorized Autobiography* (New York: HarperCollins, 1992), 51.

113 **"An intense, wiry,** John Gruen, *The Party's Over Now* (New York: Viking Press, 1972), 131.

113 **I feel repulsed** Larry Rivers's memoir (*What Did I Do? The Unauthorized Autobiography*, New York: HarperCollins, 1992) describes a household in which there was incest and sexual abuse. He said he was molested at age six by an eleven-year-old boy (p. 114) and lost his virginity in a series of what he calls "gang bangs" with a girl he describes as "short, fat," and "retarded" (p. 14). He said he tried to have sex with his mother-in-law Berdie, whom he later painted in the nude for one of his most acclaimed paintings and who served as a kind of den mother for the New York School scene (p. 74).

115 **He was so simple** Larry Rivers, with Carol Brightman, "The Cedar Bar," *New York*, November 5, 1979, 40.

116 **"a square from New Jersey"** Maxine Groffsky, interview with the author, July 1, 2021. I was pleased that Groffsky, then eighty-five, spoke with me, because she is wary of the press. On our call, she quoted de Kooning as saying on a visit to her office after he'd done a *Life* magazine interview: "You know what journalists do? They take the shit out of your mouth and they throw it in your face."

116 **The art, the energy** I imagine that would have been especially true after dating Philip Roth.

116 **"sensationally inaccurate account"** John Gruen, *The Party's Over Now* (New York: Viking Press, 1972), 138–9.

117 **"You know a major artist** Michael Shnayerson, "Crimes of the Art?" *Vanity Fair*, November 3, 2010.

117 **The *New York Times* story** Peter Haldeman, "Her Father's Daughter: The Turbulent Life of Lisa de Kooning," *New York Times*, March 15, 2013.

117 **"To the Harbormaster,"** Lucas Matthiessen was convinced the beautiful poem "The Harbormaster" must have been about Vincent Warren

and was disappointed to learn from my father that it was about Larry Rivers. See also Olivia Cole, "The Poem Stuck in My Head: Frank O'Hara's 'To the Harbormaster,'" *Paris Review*, December 15, 2011.

119 **Born in 1953 Paris** Peter Matthiessen was also later revealed to have briefly been a CIA spy. Jeff Wheelwright, "A Writer's Controversial Past That Will Not Die," *New York Times*, February 2, 2018.

120 **Matthiessen remembers O'Hara** Elaine de Kooning told Amei Wallach she knew about the relationship. Still, when the baby, Lisa, was born, she went to the hospital to see it and was wounded to discover that Ward had been admitted under the name de Kooning. Amei Wallach interview with Elaine de Kooning, March 17, 1988, 64–65.

121 **Matthiessen remembers Larry Rivers** Larry Rivers, "Speech Read at Frank O'Hara's Funeral, Springs, Long Island, July 27, 1966," in *Homage to Frank O'Hara*, eds. Bill Berkson and Joe LeSueur (Berkeley: Creative Arts Book Company, 1980), 138.

122 **Peter Orlovsky** This seemed pretty outlandish, and it was a child's recollection, so I contacted the Allen Ginsberg estate to see if it could be substantiated. I was told that it was the kind of behavior more commonly associated with "the 1980s Peter than the 1960s Peter, but it could totally be true!"

123 **According to the article I find,** Constance Rosenblum, "Love Story in Residence," *New York Times*, June 8, 2012.

126 **"My oldest granddaughter,** Julie Haifley, "Oral History Interview with Grace Hartigan," Smithsonian Archives of American Art, May 10, 1979.

127 **Gregory LaFayette was a blond actor** "Gregory LaFayette," IMDb. https://www.imdb.com/name/nm0480746/?ref_=fn_al_nm_1.

128 **"Or he'd put bourbon** This is a common story, but other versions I've heard identify his morning liquor as vodka.

129 **He was living on Broadway** According to Elaine de Kooning, when she left her studio in that building, Donald Droll moved in and then Frank O'Hara moved in on the floor above. A big 1963 party Donald Droll threw for Edwin Denby used both apartments.

141 **And I came to 'To the Art Profession,'** Vincent Katz is talking about the poem "Dear Profession of Art Writing," which appears in Peter Schjeldahl, *Since 1964: New and Selected Poems* (New York: Sun Press, 1978), 12. It begins, "My crummy benefactor, how can I not be grateful?"

144 **a verse from an eighth-century play.** Bhavabhūti, Mālatīmādhava 1.6. Unpublished translation by Josephine Brill, University of Chicago, email to the author, May 20, 2020.

146 **Malcolm writes** Janet Malcolm, *The Silent Woman: Sylvia Plath and Ted Hughes* (New York: Knopf, 1995), 8–9.

147 **"When I painted Frank O'Hara,** Elaine de Kooning quote from *Art in America* (1975), printed with image of the painting in *Homage to Frank O'Hara*, eds. Bill Berkson and Joe LeSueur (Berkeley: Creative Arts Book Company, 1980), 97.

147 **I asked if I could** As it turned out, my son got sick the day before I was planning to go to Connecticut, so I postponed my trip.

149 **She is a wonderful person** When asked about this, Amei Wallach told me: "Maureen [Granville-Smith]'s characterization is inside out. What drew me to Frank O'Hara was indeed the intersection of art and poetry, his relationships with art and artists, and his role as curator at MoMA. My first visit with de Kooning in Springs, for instance, was to interview him about Frank. Ditto Joan Mitchell, Grace Hartigan, and artists of that generation. I was earnestly educating myself in New York School poetry and poets but got lost in the brutal politics of the poetry world. And I came to feel inadequate in understanding precisely the intricacies of the social life that Maureen dismisses as my focus. I cannot imagine where she got that idea since it is so far off the mark." Email to the author, July 2, 2021.

149 **Maxine Groffsky called me** Maxine Groffsky told me she does not remember any of the conversations she may have had with Granville-Smith.

151 **All the people you listed** The people I mentioned hoping to speak with, in addition to Maureen Granville-Smith, were Katie Schneeman, Alice Notley, Lewis Warsh, Bill Zavatsky, Maxine Groffsky, Kenward Elmslie, Alex Katz, Tony Towle, Ned Rorem, Lucas Matthiessen, Larry Osgood, and Ron Padgett.

159 **"There are stories** James Salter, *Burning the Days: Recollection* (New York: Vintage International, 1997), 215.

160 **"I think at the root** Robert Storr, "On Art and Artists: Peter Schjeldahl," *Profile 3*, no. 4 (July 1983), cover.

160 **"Perhaps, on closer examination,** Christopher Isherwood, *Kathleen and Frank: The Autobiography of a Family* (New York: Farrar, Straus and Giroux, 1971), 510.

160 **I gather that there will** See, for example, the Janet Malcolm books *The Journalist and the Murderer* and *The Silent Woman*.

160 **"Why is it worth recording?** Helen Vendler, "The Virtues of the Alterable," *Parnassus: Poetry in Review* 1, no. 1 (1972): 8.

161 **"careful attention to misattribution** Frank O'Hara, *Art Chronicles, 1954–1966* (New York: George Braziller, 1975), 149. Also mentioned in Amei Wallach's interview with Elaine de Kooning, March 17, 1988, 36.

161 **Elaine quoted her mother:** Frank O'Hara, *Art Chronicles, 1954–1966* (New York: George Braziller, 1975), 155.

162 **"How can we get at it** Henry James, *The Aspern Papers* (Mineola, NY: Dover Publications, 2001), 51.

163 **"There is no 'always.'** Ted Loos, "Art/Architecture; Helen Frankenthaler, Back to the Future," *New York Times*, April 27, 2003.

170 **It's the most profound pun** Frank O'Hara, "Olive Garden," in *The Collected Poems of Frank O'Hara*, ed. Donald Allen (Berkeley: University of California Press, 1995), 92.

173 **I had to sign two contracts** For permission to use these six lines in the audiobook and in print for countries excluding the U.S., Canada, and the Philippines, I paid Curtis Brown, Ltd., $195.37. For print rights in the U.S., Canada, and the Philippines, I paid Penguin Random House $90.

176 **"What is a bar?** Larry Rivers, with Carol Brightman, "The Cedar Bar," *New York*, November 5, 1979, 39.

182 **"Who but the dead know** Morton Feldman, "Frank O'Hara: Lost Times and Future Hopes," *Art in America*, March–April 1972, 55. My father has two articles in this issue, one about James Rosenquist and the other about Vito Acconci. Irving Sandler has one about Hans Hoffman.

189 **"bracing, empowering study . . .** *"Why We Can't Sleep: Women's New Midlife Crisis,"* PublishersWeekly.com, October 18, 2019.

196 **"If I knew the world was to end** Martin Luther probably didn't say it, though. Jordan Ballor, "Luther's Apocryphal Apple Tree," *Calvinist International*, May 6, 2013.

196 **"That by desiring** George Eliot, *Middlemarch* (Knoxville, TN: Wordsworth Editions, 1994), 323.

197 **"He welcomes whatever is incomplete,** Geoffrey O'Brien, "The Mayakovsky of MacDougal Street," *New York Review of Books*, December 2, 1993.

202 **Take no prisoners.** John Ashbery, "Prisoner's Base," in *Chinese Whispers* (New York: Open Road Media, 2014).

206 **"as at the beach,** Frank O'Hara, *What's with Modern Art?* (Austin, TX: Mike and Dale's Press, 1999), 29.

209 *My daughter Ada has told me* Peter Schjeldahl, "'77 Sunset Me," *New Yorker*, December 23, 2019.

213 **"Oh, no, she suffered** My aunt Ann told me she wanted to make sure Oliver knew that what my father said about Grammy suffering was false. "Hospice made sure she was comfortable with medication. She spent that last twenty-four hours at our house, with Pip [Ann's Boston terrier] and me by her side with her saying, over and over again: 'I love

253

you, I love you . . .' When Peter showed up, she lightened up noticeably and, directly after he said, 'I love you,' she died." Ann also told me that in the sixties my father took her to a party and Larry Rivers made a pass at her.

214 **We talked about a controversial book**   Kent Johnson, *A Question Mark Above the Sun* (Buffalo, NY: Starcherone Books, 2012).

217 **"Anyone who chose Goneril**   Frank O'Hara, *Art Chronicles, 1954–1966* (New York: George Braziller, 1975), 155.

222 **"As women,**   Audre Lorde, "Uses of the Erotic: The Erotic as Power" (1978), in *The Selected Works of Audre Lorde* (New York: W. W. Norton, 2020), 31.

229 **In Frank O'Hara's "Rhapsody,"**   Frank O'Hara, "Rhapsody," *Evergreen Review* 10, no. 43, October 1966, 29.

About the Author

New York Times–bestselling author Ada Calhoun has written for the *New York Times*; *O, The Oprah Magazine*; and the *New Republic*. Her previous books include *St. Marks Is Dead*; *Wedding Toasts I'll Never Give*; and *Why We Can't Sleep*, an *Indie Next* pick and one of the best nonfiction books of 2020 according to Amazon's editors. She lives in New York City.

Acknowledgments

After reading the first draft of this book, my father wrote me an email in which he said: "I had a passing and then a returning thought that it's the best book I ever read." I was relieved, grateful, and surprised.

Then again, the past two years have been nothing if not surprising. Would the rough parts have been tolerable without my husband, Neal; son, Oliver; and stepson, Andrew Blake? I doubt it. They are three terrific human beings, and as of this year they are all much taller than me.

My agent, Daniel Greenberg, fellow East Village kid, is fiercely protective, wryly funny, and a next-level problem solver. I am so lucky to have him and his colleague Tim Wojcik in my corner.

Audible, which also published the audiobook of my last book, *Why We Can't Sleep*, called dibs early on the audio of this project and I'm so glad. Jessica Almond Galland is a brilliant editor and a lovely person, and I am grateful for the chance to work with her again. Thanks also to the whole team at Audible, especially Esther Bochner, David Blum, Kristin Lang, and Don Katz. I'm so grateful, too, that they sent the brilliant lawyer John Pelosi and the intrepid Girl Friday Productions fact-checkers my way.

ACKNOWLEDGMENTS

That Grove Press, which published Frank O'Hara's *Meditations in an Emergency*, wanted to work together again so soon after my last book was a godsend. The publisher's history of bravery and creativity is embodied today by my tenacious young editor, Katie Raissian. Thanks for the care and attention shown by everyone in that house, from meticulous copyeditor Paula Cooper Hughes to the designers to the sales reps to Judy Hottensen, Deb Seager, Amy Hundley, Peter Blackstock, Julia Berner-Tobin, Morgan Entrekin, Elisabeth Schmitz, Andrew Unger, Becca Fox, Sal Destro, Alicia Burns, and Justina Batchelor. They also throw great parties.

Several wise people gave early versions of this book their thoughtful attention: Neal Medlyn (an excellent editor in addition to being a first-rate husband), Susannah Cahalan, Carlene Bauer, Jason Zinoman, Tara McKelvey, Abbott Kahler, Maureen Callahan, my aunt Ann Morris, and Asia Wong (thirty-eight years into this friendship, I still can't imagine ever being bored in your presence). Special thanks to Kathleen Hanna for taking my author photo and serving as my book-tour entourage of one.

Among the great joys in my life: letters from my two O'Hara-esque pen pals; readings with my journalism gang Sob Sisters; games with my low-stakes Power Broker poker club (Miner's Headlamp 4EVR); screenwriting with Busy Philipps; Easter with my godchildren; hermeneutics with my favorite Sanskritists, Jo Brill and Deven Patel; pandemic grocery packing at the Union Pool food bank; minigolf with Murray Hill; trivia nights with Nola Macek; coffee with Lili Taylor; Don Waring's sermons at Grace Church; Invisible Institute meetings; martinis with Tim Gunn; and conversations with my miraculous shrink, Amy Jordan Jones.

While writing this book, I asked a lot of smart people dumb questions. For their stories, expertise, and generosity of spirit, I'd like to thank Josh Schneiderman, Katie Schneeman, Ron Padgett, Karen

Koch, Amei Wallach, Connie Lewallen, Maxine Groffsky, Keith McDermott, and Vincent Katz.

I don't usually change names in nonfiction, but Spencer was an innocent civilian caught in family crossfire, so in his case I have. Yet again, he is "kind of extra special."

For photo permissions, thank you to the great James Hamilton for the portraits of my father and me; and to Renate Ponsold (and Michael Hecht), for letting us use her iconic image of Frank O'Hara with his typewriter.

For their extreme goodness, I owe a debt to the friends and neighbors who helped my parents during and after the fire, including Ulli Barta, George Trakas, Linda Dunne, Scott Hill, Beverly Archer, Rita Devine, and EV Grieve (who issued an all-points bulletin to help find their lost cat)—and to those who helped save their stuff, especially Guy Richards Smit, Atelier 4, Lisa Rosen, Paper Conservation Studio, and Jane Curley. Thanks also to Memorial Sloan Kettering Cancer Center's Kent Sepkowitz, Gregory Riely, and Aimee-Lauren Rosales.

Before the coronavirus closed it, the Allen Room of the New York Public Library was my cave of choice. Thank you, Melanie Locay, for the opportunity to work in the classiest writing room in the world. And a special shoutout to librarians everywhere for taking such good care of me and my books. In the same spirit: a warm hello to the independent bookstore people who have sold my books and hosted my events over the years. I don't write *just* so I'll have an excuse to hang out with you, but maybe a little.

My mother's support of this project has been a great gift. Most of all, of course, thanks to my father. When I said I was afraid of what he'd think of what I'd written, he told me: "I hope I never confuse truth with a back rub." I like to think that for him and for me this book wound up, in some strange way, being both.